Martyn Payne joined the *Barnabas* team in January 2003, having wor
Children's Work Co-ordinator for several years. Martyn has wide experience of working with
schools to explore ways of opening up the Bible with children.

Before his time with CMS, Martyn worked for eighteen years as a teacher in East London, both
leading a modern languages department and also involved in the planning, writing and delivery of
RE lessons. He has experience in producing materials for schools and has produced a large bank of
flexible outlines, which have been widely used in the classroom.

Martyn has travelled in Europe, the Middle East and Africa, where he has also been involved in
training children's workers and teachers. Martyn is an experienced workshop leader, Godly Play
teacher and speaker and has collaborated with children's advisers and education officers in major
school and family events across the UK. Based in London, he is available to lead training sessions,
take workshops and help run special events throughout the UK.

✱

Betty Pedley was Parish Education Adviser (Children) in the Missionary Diocese of Wakefield for ten
years before taking up her current role as a parish priest near Halifax in Yorkshire. She has written
a great deal of material to help parishes in communicating the Christian faith with their children,
and she has a special interest in all-age worship and learning. Before ordination she worked as a
teacher and for a number of years was head of a special needs support service. Betty is an Honorary
Canon of Wakefield Cathedral.

Text copyright © Martyn Payne and Betty Pedley 2004
Illustrations copyright © Jane Taylor 2004
The author asserts the moral right
to be identified as the author of this work

Published by
The Bible Reading Fellowship
First Floor, Elsfield Hall
15–17 Elsfield Way, Oxford OX2 8FG

ISBN 1 84101 264 5
First published 2004
10 9 8 7 6 5 4 3 2 1 0

Acknowledgments
Unless otherwise stated, scripture quotations are taken from the Contemporary
English Version of the Bible published by HarperCollins Publishers, copyright
© 1991, 1992, 1995 American Bible Society.

Scriptures quoted from the Good News Bible published by The Bible
Societies/HarperCollins Publishers Ltd, UK © American Bible Society 1966,
1971, 1976, 1992, used with permission.

Extracts from The Book of Common Prayer of 1662, the rights of which are
vested in the Crown in perpetuity within the United Kingdom, are reproduced by
permission of Cambridge University Press, Her Majesty's Printers.

A catalogue record for this book is available from the British Library

Printed and bound in Malta

A-CROSS
the world

An exploration of forty representations of the cross
from the worldwide Christian Church

Martyn Payne and Betty Pedley

Acknowledgments

BRF and CMS wish to acknowledge and thank the people and organizations that gave us permission to reproduce material during the compiling of the stories and information for this book. Every effort has been made to trace the sources and copyrights of all other material.

In particular, thanks go to:

Angela Ashwin for the prayers to use with the holding cross.

John Carden for the prayer on page 114, taken from A Procession of Prayers, compiled and edited by John Carden and published by Cassell.

It has proved impossible to trace the origin of some of the prayers. Should readers have information as to the source of some of the unaccredited material, CMS and BRF would be grateful to hear from them.

Our thanks also go to all those CMS staff, Mission Partners, Children's Advisers and teachers who helped to gather and test out the material over a number of years; to Sue Doggett of BRF for her encouragement and advice in turning the original CMS folder into this extended book format; and also to the editing and design staff at BRF for their patience and thorough sifting of the often complex material.

Finally, particular thanks must go to Joyce McCaulsky of CMS, who patiently and faithfully typed and arranged the original version of this book. Without her prayerful encouragement, A-cross the World might never have seen the light of day!

Contents

Crosses from Europe

PART TWO: USING THE CROSSES WITH YOUR GROUP OR CLASS

Appendix

Foreword

For most people, the cross is a familiar symbol. Yet we can easily forget that it is so much more than a classic design for a pendant or a common feature of a skyline view. It tells a story, one of a gruesome execution that has nevertheless been greeted by many as a triumph rather than a tragic failure. This is a story that has had an impact on the lives of millions over the past two thousand years. It is a story that continues to inspire and shape the lives of individuals and societies around the globe.

This imaginative resource book, *A-cross the World*, offers fascinating insights into this story, its origins and the variety of ways in which its meaning has been understood by Christians throughout the world. By examining the ways the cross is depicted, we uncover further stories about the diverse communities for whom the story of the cross of Jesus Christ is at the heart of their faith.

The depiction of the cross commonly associated with Archbishops of Canterbury is the Canterbury cross. The original Canterbury cross, dating from around AD850, was excavated in 1867 in St George's Street in Canterbury. In this resource book, it features only in the Appendix. But it is a modest example of the type of associations, often hidden to most of us, which we encounter through this book. There is a great deal to learn from this highly practical and illuminating volume.

+ Rowan Cantuar
Archbishop of Canterbury

How to use this book

The world family of those who follow the Christian faith crosses many boundaries of culture, colour and nationality. Nevertheless, whether it be the traditional churches of Western Europe or the ancient fellowships of the Middle East, the indigenous communities of faith springing up in Asia or the local congregations of Africa, the Orthodox cathedrals of Eastern Europe or the emerging base-communities of Latin America, there is one sign that they all hold in common—the cross. This is often the one unifying symbol for these diverse groups of Christian believers and yet even this very cross has often been adapted, decorated or interpreted to convey a particular story of its own. This book seeks to explore some of these stories, along with ideas for special events in churches, project work and assemblies in schools, including craft ideas that groups can follow, should they wish to produce their own versions of these crosses for display.

Since the material in this book was first published in a ringbinder format by the Church Mission Society (CMS) in 2001, it has been welcomed and widely used both in schools and in churches throughout the country. This book edition from BRF and CMS aims to make the material even more well-known and available and includes fifteen new crosses as well as a wealth of new suggestions as to how to use this resource with groups in schools, churches or as part of worship.

The book is in two sections. Part One contains the stories of forty different crosses from around the world. Each one includes:

• A Bible link, with some wondering questions
• A craft idea for making a similar cross
• Information about the life of the Christian Church in that part of the world

Part Two contains the following material for leaders so that they can put together ideas for special events and for particular situations:

• Outline for a two-hour programme
• Ideas for a holiday club

• Ideas for all-age worship
• Ideas for collective worship at Key Stages One and Two
• Bible activities for small groups
• Further cross designs and ideas

The raw material for these sessions is grouped in the opening pages of Part Two under the following headings:

• Icebreakers
• Games
• Prayers, poems and quotations
• Craft ideas
• Spoken theme prayers
• Visual prayers
• Key words for the crosses

There are then outlines and worked examples of different sorts of presentations, showing how the material can be organized and used. They include:

• An outline for a two-hour special programme along with two worked examples
• A holiday club outline
• An outline for all-age worship, including a calendar of dates for festivals linked to particular countries and crosses
• Outlines for collective worship at Key Stages One and Two

The final part of this section offers a series of small-group activities linked to the meaning of the cross as discovered through various Bible stories.

In the appendix you will find:

• Guidelines for events involving children
• Information about CMS and BRF
• Further cross designs and ideas for crosses

The material in this book has come together over a number of years, during which it was tried and tested in a wide range of events with children. The authors hope that this volume will inspire many more such events to take place in our schools and churches and that it will help children, with their teachers and leaders, to think again about the meaning of the cross and why it is such an important and enduring symbol for Christians all around the world.

We hope you will enjoy using *A-cross the World*. BRF and CMS would be very happy to hear how you have used this material. The authors are very aware that this collection of crosses and the information linked to them is by no means exhaustive. We are sure that you will be inspired to find and develop your own ideas as you discover and work with other crosses, which have either local or global connections. However, by sharing these stories in churches and in schools, it is hoped that the experience Christians have of God's love for the whole world and of his continuing mission to 'the people of all nations' will be better known and understood.

Introduction:
Cross reference

A UNIVERSAL SYMBOL

Around the world today the cross is, arguably, the one universally recognized symbol of the Christian faith. It is carried high in liturgical procession, it is worn prominently as jewellery or ornamentation, and the sign of the cross is made to bless the faithful or to ward off evil. The cross defines the shape of the lowliest Christian church and sits atop the steeple of the grandest cathedral. Whether made of stone or wood, marble or precious metal, the cross signifies to the world the central event in the story of Jesus Christ—an event that, for Christians, stands as the turning-point in human history. It was the moment when a holy God of love made it possible for unholy people to be reunited with their creator. It was the moment when death's full stop was turned into a comma for those who believe. It was the moment when a high and mighty God tasted the full horror of the worst that human beings can do to each other.

THE HISTORIC CROSS

It was not always the case, however, that the sign of the cross was so universally used by the Christian Church. The cross itself is, of course, quite crudely an execution post. It was an instrument of torture and death that the Roman empire had adopted as its particular means of public punishment, setting an example of humiliating agony that was designed to enforce its rule of law. The Romans had taken this form of execution from the Phoenicians and used three types of cross: a cross shaped like a capital T (the *crux commissa*), sometimes called the tau cross or St Anthony's cross; a cross shaped like a capital X (the *crux decussata*), sometimes called St Andrew's

cross; or the more familiar Latin cross with its two beams (the *crux immissa*), which is probably the one used to crucify Jesus, since reference is made in the Gospels to the board, on which the words 'This is Jesus, the King of the Jews' were written, fixed above his head.

Although crucifixion is a most painful form of death, the writers of the New Testament do not describe Jesus' physical suffering in great detail. They are more interested in the eternal meaning of Jesus' death and its consequences. The cross itself soon came to represent symbolically the rescue story that God had accomplished in Christ.

In the Old Testament, bodies of executed criminals were sometimes hung on a tree as a grim warning to others. To be hung up like that was therefore seen as being under a curse. Early Christians saw that as being true for Jesus, whom they believed was cursed on behalf of the whole human race for all the wrong that we did. This view explains the description of the cross as the 'tree' or 'tree of shame'. Perhaps because of its association with shameful death, the first Christian communities tended not to use the cross as a sign of their victorious new faith.

Instead they preferred secret signs or symbols—images such as the fish (*ichthus*, Greek for 'fish', the initial letters of which in Greek are a mnemonic for 'Jesus Christ Son of God Saviour'); the Chi-Ro (the first two Greek letters of 'Christ') or the shepherd and the lamb (a favourite image taken from Jesus' own description of himself in the Gospel of John). The first Christians liked to 'hide' the cross design within another important symbol of the faith. The best example of this is the Anchor cross (see p. 155). In the New Testament, Christian hope in Jesus is referred to as a sure anchor for life (Hebrews 6:19).

The Emperor Constantine abolished crucifixion in the Roman empire in AD315 and this led to the gradual acceptance of the cross by believers as the main symbol of their faith. In AD325 the Council of Nicaea made the cross the official symbol of Christianity. With this acceptance came an increasing interest in exactly what the cross of Christ was like, and many claims were made about its whereabouts. Helena, the mother of the emperor, for example, claimed to have found the true cross on one of her journeys to the Holy Land. Throughout Christian history there have been countless so-called pieces of the 'true' cross, sold as religious relics.

THE CROSS OR THE CRUCIFIX

In the early centuries of the Church, Christians were very wary of making any representation of Jesus' physical appearance. The early believers' Jewish roots and their adherence to the commandment not to make any 'graven image' ensured that there were very few early pictures of Jesus. It was in this context that the cross gradually became a symbol (one of several) of the faith. Many of the early crosses, rather than displaying the body of Christ as part of their design, showed a lamb above or below the cross—a reference to Jesus as 'the Lamb of God'.

In time, however, the quest for the true likeness of Jesus did lead to various representations of Christ, fuelled by visions and miraculous relics such as the Veronica cloth, which was a likeness of Jesus said to have been imprinted on a cloth handed to him by St Veronica during their brief encounter as Jesus stumbled his way to the cross.

These representations led, in turn, to portrayals of Christ on the cross, and in the course of Christian history tensions have often arisen between those who preferred the crucifix (a cross with the figure of Christ on it) to the empty cross as a symbol of their faith. Perhaps a more helpful approach is to recognize the need for both these symbols—the first reminding believers how Jesus totally encompassed in himself the suffering of the human race, with the second emphasizing the empty tomb and the truth of his resurrection.

A-CROSS THE WORLD

Thus the cross has become a focus of faith for Christians. Throughout history, many individuals and religious orders have adopted particular designs of the cross as symbols of special significance to them. There are, therefore, many versions of the cross that have become associated with particular saints or religious movements. This practice of creating a 'special cross' continues today. Different indigenous churches all over the world have taken the same simple cross and, using local art and cultural artefacts, have turned it into a symbol that expresses their own experiences of the faith. In this way each cross speaks about the unity of believers, which links the many diverse cultures and also provides special insight into, and understanding of, God. Each cross thereby contributes to the big picture of God's love for the whole world.

THE CROSS WE SHARE

The aim of this resource is to present an overview and examples of a collection of crosses that are shared by the Christian family worldwide and to offer background on the crosses as a help to the churches and schools in this country. It aims to be a contribution to the understanding of the Christian faith and, for some, a means by which that faith can develop and deepen.

In order to give you an opportunity for further reflection and to enable you to discuss this important symbol, the book also contains suggestions for making a version of each of the crosses, using various craft techniques. Churches, schools and study groups that have already used the first version of some of this material have found this to be a helpful way to reflect on these symbols and a means of appreciating the rich contribution that we can receive from the worldwide Church. Schools have used the material to explore the use of symbol to express faith within different cultures. Church groups have used the resource as a basis for Good Friday workshops or for special mission weekends. The material also lends itself to banner-making and to displays that celebrate Christian links across the world.

The book also contains a wealth of further ideas and potential activities for exploring the meaning of the cross for Christians today, particularly for sharing it with children and in the context of all-age worship, special children's events, lessons and corporate worship in schools as well as in small midweek groups.

By no means does the resource give an exhaustive list of the very many crosses and cross designs that exist worldwide. We have drawn upon links with the Church overseas in order to put together this collection and we are always eager to hear of other cultural expressions of the cross that can further enrich an understanding of the Christian faith and encourage the proclaiming of 'the good news of the cross' to the world.

As a stimulus for discussion and an inspiration for display work, the forty crosses explored in this book are available to view on the BRF website www.brf.org.uk.

PART ONE

Crosses from around the world

An Ethiopian cross

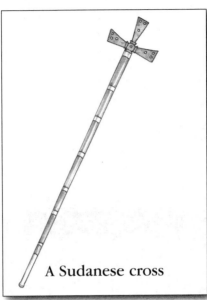

A Sudanese cross

An Egyptian cross

A mid-African cross

An African crucifix

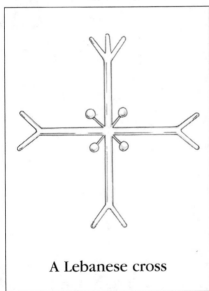

A Lebanese cross

A palm cross

An Iranian cross

The Jerusalem cross

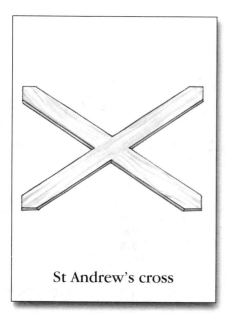

St Andrew's cross

A South Indian cross

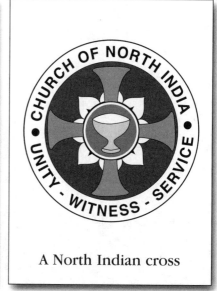

A North Indian cross

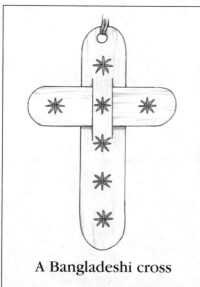

A Bangladeshi cross

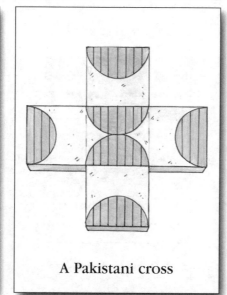

A Pakistani cross

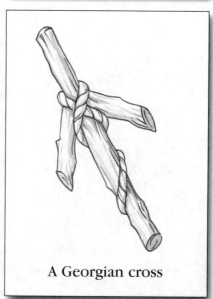

A Georgian cross

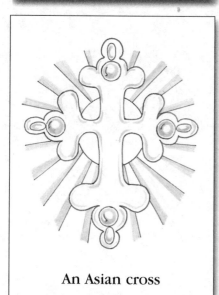

An Asian cross

A Korean cross

A Chinese cross

A Japanese cross

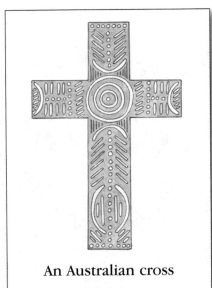

An Australian cross

A Salvadorean cross

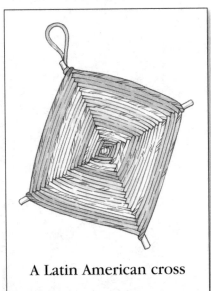

A Latin American cross

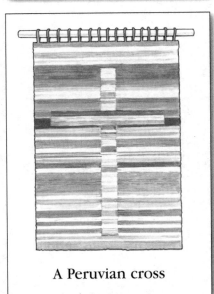

A Peruvian cross

An Orthodox cross

A Celtic cross

The Taizé cross

An Irish cross

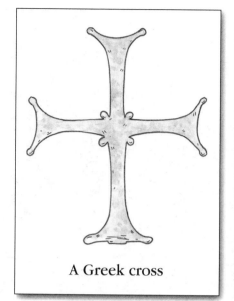

A Greek cross

A Finnish cross

A Maltese cross

A Roman cross

An Italian cross

A Swiss cross

A cross of nails

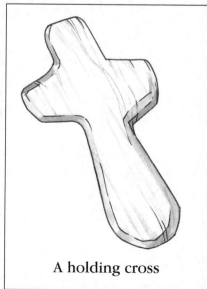

A holding cross

A partnership cross

St Alban's cross

St Martin's cross

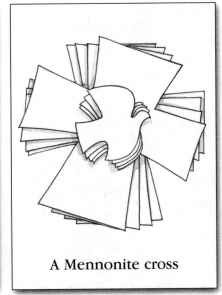

A Mennonite cross

A Bible cross

An Ethiopian cross

was silent as a lamb whose wool is being cut off...' The official said to Philip, 'Tell me, was the prophet talking about himself or about someone else?' So Philip began at this place in the Scriptures and explained the good news about Jesus.

This is the story of the first Ethiopian Christian, a minister in the government, who met the evangelist Philip as he was travelling home from Jerusalem.

Wondering about this Bible story

- I wonder what Philip told the official about the cross of Jesus?
- I wonder what the official said to the queen when he eventually arrived back at her court?
- I wonder whether he ever met Philip again?

Bible link: Acts 8:26–35

The Lord's angel said to Philip, 'Go south along the desert road that leads from Jerusalem to Gaza.' So Philip left. An important Ethiopian official happened to be going along that road in his chariot. He was the chief treasurer for Candace, the Queen of Ethiopia. The official had gone to Jerusalem to worship and was now on his way home. He was sitting in his chariot, reading the book of the prophet Isaiah. The Spirit told Philip to catch up with the chariot. Philip ran up close and heard the man reading aloud from the book of Isaiah. Philip asked him, 'Do you understand what you are reading?' The official answered, 'How can I understand unless someone helps me?' He then invited Philip to come up and sit beside him. The man was reading the passage that said, 'He was led like a sheep on its way to be killed. He

The story of this cross

According to one tradition, St Matthew first brought the gospel to Ethiopia, though others link its first appearance there to the conversion of the royal treasurer who met the evangelist Philip while travelling back from a visit to Jerusalem (see the Bible link).

Ethiopia became a Christian state in AD332, when the emperor of the kingdom of Axum, as Ethiopia was then called, responded to the preaching of two shipwrecked young men, Frumentius and Edesius, from Syria. Frumentius went on to become the first archbishop of the region and took the title of 'Abba Salama', a title still used to this day. The Ethiopian Orthodox Church is one of the most ancient national churches in the world and the third largest in the Orthodox tradition after those of Russia and Romania. About half of Ethiopia's population are members of this church.

Church services are held early on Sunday mornings. They generally use the ancient Geez language of northern Ethiopia, although modern, everyday Ethiopian (Amharic) is being used increasingly for parts of the liturgy. Church buildings are usually circular and have roofs of thatch or corrugated iron. At Lalibela, in the north of the country, there are eleven churches dug out of the rock, which date from the 13th century and are still in use today.

Along with its historic neighbour, the Coptic Orthodox Church of Egypt, the Ethiopian Orthodox Church is under pressure and its members are, as on many occasions in their history, tolerated rather than valued by the government.

There is a rich tradition in the Ethiopian Orthodox Church of training special singers and musicians from a very young age to contribute to the worship. The scriptures are chanted from memory by *dabtara*, as these young vocalists and instrumentalists are called. These boys are given responsibilities within communal worship and are even known as junior deacons.

There are many stories about the early Christian pioneers in Ethiopia, and pictures of these saints are preserved on church murals and in religious artwork. One picture at the church on Mount Zuquala is very early evidence that war and drought—features of life in this region in recent years—are not purely modern

phenomena. In the picture, St Raguel is praying for peace, symbolized by the lion and the lamb lying at his feet. He is also crying for his country, which is suffering a severe drought, and a bird has come to drink the saint's tears in order to quench its thirst.

The Ethiopian cross is sometimes also called the Axum cross, derived from the original name of Aksumis, which is a religious centre of Ethiopian Coptic Christians in northern Ethiopia. The shape and variety of the crosses used within it are distinctive features of the Christian Church in Ethiopia. There are handheld crosses, usually made of wood, which are used to bless worshippers; processional crosses, which are very elaborate in design and made of metal; pendant crosses; and special crosses that adorn church buildings.

The basic Ethiopian cross takes the form of a circle with the cross set inside it. Some Ethiopian crosses are designed in rhombus shapes and have vegetable motifs, which are links to the narrative of the garden of Eden and the tree of life. There is sometimes a square tablet, which may contain words or occasionally a picture, at the base of some of these crosses. Triangles, details of flowers and various zigzag patterns are also very common in different makes of this cross.

The Ethiopian Orthodox Church is well known for its ornate metal and wooden crosses. Apart from the crosses worn by individual Christians, churches have their own processional versions and all priests carry small hand crosses, which are reverently kissed by the faithful. Some women even have magnificent crosses temporarily tattooed on to their faces at festival times.

The large processional crosses are very striking, with their ornate metal patterns and the brightly coloured cloths that usually hang down from the latticework. The designs are often complex and colourful, reflecting the craftsman's desire to indicate that, for believers, the cross is a symbol of vibrancy and life and not just a place of death.

One of the most important feasts of the Ethiopian church year is *Mesquel* in September, which is the Festival of the True Cross. It is celebrated in both Western and Eastern traditions and commemorates the traditional finding of the true cross in Jerusalem by St Helena, the mother of the Emperor Constantine. In Ethiopia there is an extra dimension, as, according to their version of the story, Helena was led to the place where the cross was buried by lighting a bonfire. As part of contemporary celebrations in Ethiopia, bonfires are lit. The ashes are later marked on the foreheads of worshippers and also spread on to the fields to ensure good crops.

The following are some words from the daily liturgy used in the Ethiopian Coptic Church.

Deacon: Pray before the cross,
All you, the faithful,
Holding it on the right
And renouncing Satan,
For it has been sanctified by the
blood of Christ the Saviour.

Congregation: Honoured art thou, O Cross, King of
woods,
Honoured art thou, O Cross.
And honoured is the blood of the
Divinity, the Word, which
Sanctified thee.

Priest: In honour of this Cross,
We Christians prostrate ourselves
with fear and awe,
For the Son Himself in person
Hath sanctified it with His blood,
not with that of others,
When, on the Cross,
Divinity died in His humanity.

Crafting the cross

A craft idea for making a similar cross

Enlarge the illustrative examples given on page 157 as templates for making your own Ethiopian decorative crosses.

- Stick the enlarged template on to some card and then carefully cut round the shape of the cross.
- Cover the cross with silver kitchen foil and smooth the foil down, folding any of its extra edges around the back of the cross and taping them down so that the foil does not peal off.
- Decorate this silver cross with beads, old buttons, sequins and glitter. Try to ensure that you make the patterns and colours symmetrical.
- Alternatively, simply colour in the templates or stick coloured wrapping-paper, cut up into lots of different shapes, on to them.

Another craft idea for creating ornate crosses in the Ethiopian style is to cut snowflake-type patterns from folded paper.

- Take a square of paper and draw a circle in the middle, using a pencil. Fold the paper in half, corner to corner, and then in half again.
- Draw two straight lines from the circle to the longest edge of the folded paper. These lines will act as your basic cutting guide.
- Add further symmetrical patterns to all three edges of the paper, as in the example below. Cut away the shaded areas and open out the paper to reveal your decorative cross.
- Different coloured papers could add a further dimension. If large versions are mounted on card, they can become paper copies of the processional crosses that are so popular in Ethiopia.

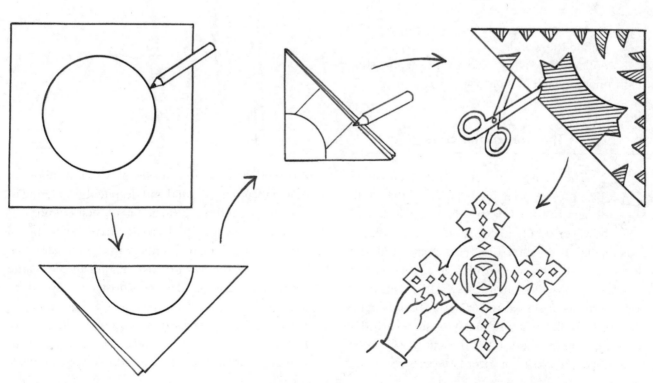

A Sudanese cross

Bible link: Lamentations 5:1–5

 Our Lord, don't forget how we have suffered and been disgraced. Foreigners and strangers have taken our land and our homes. We are like children whose mothers are widows. The water we drink and the wood we burn cost far too much. We are terribly ill-treated; we are worn out and can find no rest.

This is from the last chapter of Jeremiah's book of weeping for the destruction of Jerusalem and the taking into exile of the people of God. Many Sudanese find the words of this sad poem very meaningful in their situation today.

Wondering about this Bible story

- I wonder where God is when things seem to go so horribly wrong?
- I wonder what God feels about all the pain in the world?
- I wonder what can be said to those who suffer through no fault of their own?

The story of this cross

The Dinka tribe of southern Sudan are proud to lift high the cross that is the sign of their Christian faith. Their cross is, however, a rather special one because of how it is made. It is carved out of ebony and then decorated with beaten bronze. To create circular bands of bronze for their crosses, the Dinka use spent cartridge cases ejected from rifle barrels or gun chambers. Sadly, there are plenty of such cartridges left lying around as a result of the war that has been tearing Sudan apart for over 40 years. Sudanese

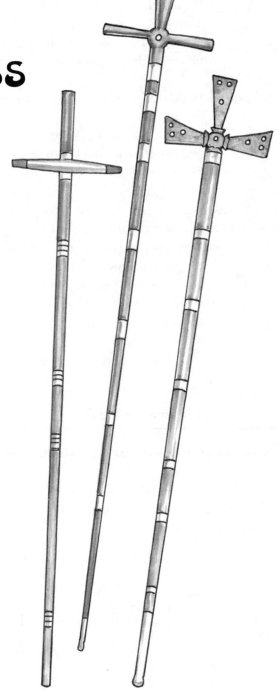

Christians carry these crosses as visual symbols of their faith and hope amid and despite the suffering of their people and the destruction of their country.

New songs and local crosses have been special features of the Sudanese church in recent years, as it has coped with massive loss of human life, cattle wealth and land. Sudanese Christians have been obliged to rely on God completely. For example, despite all the setbacks they have met, members of the Episcopal Church of Sudan challenge us with their cry, 'But God is not defeated!' The old animistic and 'magic powers' that once held such influential sway over the Sudanese people have been largely rejected and their symbols turned into finely crafted crosses of ebony or mahogany decorated with brass and ivory. These individual crosses are often linked to their owners' stories of survival and faith. There are several pictures of such Sudanese crosses on the BRF website.

One young man called Makuel, who took the name Philip when he was baptized, made a remarkable cross. Using metal from the wreckage of a MIG jet fighter that had been shot down near his home, he created a cross from the very object that had brought death and terror to his people. The shape that Makuel created captured a collision of the noses of four jet fighters. At the point of 'contact' between them, he has carved the person of Christ. So the power of death is again challenged and transformed into a victory for life. The Reverend Marc Nikkel was instrumental in making this and the story of other Sudanese crosses well-known in the UK. As a joint mission partner of CMS and the Episcopal Church of the USA, Marc worked tirelessly to come alongside and understand the plight of Sudanese Christians and to work with them in their struggles.

More information on this cross and the wider story of the Sudanese church can be found in *But God Is Not Defeated!* edited by Samuel Kayanga and Andrew Wheeler, published by Paulines Publications Africa and available through CMS. This book was published to celebrate the centenary of the Episcopal Church of Sudan in 1999.

Crafting the cross

A craft idea for making a similar cross

You will need:
- ✠ Garden cane, at least 26cm long
- ✠ Insulating or reflector tape in two different colours: bright yellow and black
- ✠ Garden twine
- ✠ Sticky tape

Cut up the cane into two lengths of 18cm and 8cm. Stick small 1.5cm strips of black tape at intervals around each length, leaving space for strips of the yellow tape to be inserted in between the black ones. Attach the 8cm crosspiece to the upright and secure it with the twine. You may find some sticky tape useful in making the join as firm as possible.

Tell the story of this cross as you do this craft activity together.

An Egyptian cross

Bible link: Matthew 2:13–15

After the wise men had gone, an angel from the Lord appeared to Joseph in a dream and said, 'Get up! Hurry and take the child and his mother to Egypt! Stay there until I tell you to return, because Herod is looking for the child and wants to kill him.' That night, Joseph got up and took his wife and the child to Egypt, where they stayed until Herod died. So the Lord's promise came true, just as the prophet had said, 'I called my son out of Egypt.'

Egypt was the first place where the child Jesus lived for any length of time. At an early age Jesus became part of a refugee family, which had fled from King Herod to live abroad among strangers.

Wondering about this Bible story

- I wonder how the holy family felt, living so far from home?
- I wonder whether Jesus remembered anything from those early years in Egypt?
- I wonder why Matthew alone of the Gospel writers records this detail of Jesus' life?

The story of this cross

The roots of the Coptic Church of Egypt can be traced right back to the first centuries of the Christian Church. Alexandria was a major Christian centre and was home to many of the founding fathers and teachers of the Christian faith. Later, the deserts of Egypt became home to many monastic communities that established themselves in such barren terrain.

Following the Muslim invasion of AD642, the Coptic Church came under intense pressure from Arab rulers. Today there is freedom of religion in Egypt but unofficial discrimination still exists. Despite this, church membership is growing, especially among the young. Services nowadays are conducted in Arabic and there has been an increase in the number of schools offering some Christian instruction. Many young Christians are choosing to enter monastic life. The production of Christian literature is on the increase. Egyptian Christians are also active in involving the church in new projects that recognize and meet the needs of the poorest in society.

Coptic worship is steeped in the Bible, and stories such as that of the three exiles being miraculously preserved in the fiery furnace (as told in Daniel 3:8–30) hold particular significance for those Christians in Egyptian society who face pressures today. Although overt missionary activity is not possible in present-day Egypt, Coptic Christians believe that by proving faithful in their worship and in the example they set in their Christian lives, they can provide a model by which new people will be drawn to the Christian faith.

The ankh is an ancient sign in existence from the times of the Pharaohs and is a symbol of the key to immortality. Although in the West it has come to be used as a symbol of New Age beliefs, many Egyptian Christians today still use the ankh as a sign that speaks to them of Jesus, the way to everlasting life made possible through the cross. Some Coptic Christians even have this cross tattooed on to their wrist when very young.

A craft idea for making a similar cross

To make your own ankh cross, photocopy this template on to card.

Cut out the shape of the ankh and then wind pipe-cleaners around the cross to give it extra body and strength. Use staples to make the ends of the pipe-cleaners sit firmly on the card.

Using pipe-cleaners in different colours would help to reflect the beauty of Orthodox worship, in which such crosses would be used.

Reproduced with permission from *A–Cross the World* published by BRF 2004 (1 84101 264 5)

A mid-African cross

Bible link: I John 1:5–7

Jesus told us that God is light and doesn't have any darkness in him. Now we are telling you. If we say that we share in life with God and keep on living in the dark, we are lying and are not living by the truth. But if we live in the light, as God does, we share in life with each other. And the blood of his Son Jesus washes all our sins away.

John reminds his readers that God is light and that Jesus is our example. Following him means that we should walk in that light and not allow darkness in any form to spoil our lives.

Wondering about this Bible story

- I wonder what this darkness is that can spoil lives?
- I wonder why John had to remind his readers about all this?
- I wonder how the blood of Jesus (i.e. the cross) can wash away all that is bad?

The story of this cross

Rwanda and Burundi are two neighbouring countries that lie at the heart of the huge continent of Africa. In the early decades of the 20th century, two CMS missionary doctors from south-west Uganda began a new work across the border in these two countries, which at the time were under Belgian colonial rule. It was in this way that the 'Rwanda mission' was born.

In the 1930s, this part of Africa was the setting for a remarkable revival movement, in which thousands of people became Christians. The revival was characterized by a new determination to 'walk in the light' in accordance with the apostle John's instructions in his first letter. In this way there would be true fellowship with one another and with God. This often led to public confession of wrongdoing by church leaders as well as whole congregations. Key teaching at the time centred around themes of prayerfulness, brokenness, fullness, openness and oneness.

There was an outpouring of new songs for worship. Perhaps the most famous was the revival hymn that begins 'Tukutendereza Yesu', which means 'Praise Jesus'. In the words of a book by Patricia St John describing this time, the movement was a 'breath of life' in central Africa.

Back in Britain, prayer and giving for Rwanda mission was high. Although The Rwandan Mission was only a small missionary society affiliated to CMS, it enjoyed much loyal support and made an enormous impact on many evangelical Christians.

In 1962, Rwanda and Burundi gained independence from Belgium. As has often been the case in Africa, the colonial rulers paid little respect to the indigenous tribal territories when drawing up country boundaries and ignored the fact that Rwanda and Burundi have populations made up of both the Hutu and the Tutsi peoples.

In the last decade of the 20th century, political unrest erupted. In Rwanda in 1994, the Hutu government initiated the slaughter of Tutsis and moderate Hutus. There followed an awful genocide that left over half a million dead, while two million fled to refugee camps in Tanzania and the Democratic Republic of Congo. Most of these refugees have since been repatriated. Sadly, similar ethnic tensions are a constant threat in the country of Burundi.

The nation of Rwanda was traumatized by what had happened and the country now faces the enormous challenge of rebuilding itself, caring for the many orphans and widows and bringing reconciliation between the different tribal groups. Prisons are still full as the authorities try to deal with the daunting task of administering justice with regard to those who are accused of being involved in the killings. Recently Rwanda has introduced a new flag and a new national anthem in an attempt to look forward to a better future.

There remains a sharp division between rich and poor in both countries, and most people survive on subsistence farming. Traditional family units have been badly affected by the genocide and sporadic violence. AIDS and economic migration to larger villages and towns along the main roads have also disrupted inherited ways of life in this beautiful rural part of Africa.

During the revival, the cross in Rwanda was the place of brokenness, where people could take the things they had done wrong and make a new start. The Christian cross has once again taken on renewed significance for the peoples of these countries following the violence and the bloodshed of recent years. The cross is the place where those who previously had been enemies can come and both offer and receive forgiveness through the grace of God. The emphasis has been on the level ground that there must be before the cross of Christ, where there

is 'neither Hutu nor Tutsi, neither rich nor poor, neither those with power nor those who are powerless'. This is a modern outworking of the New Testament teaching found in Galatians 3:26–28.

The church is also renewing its efforts to meet the physical, social and spiritual needs of the people. Christians are involved in reconciliation, offering support and guidance to a broken people, who are seeking healing and forgiveness.

Rwanda Mission changed its name to Mid-Africa Ministry and as such has recently been integrated again into CMS as one society working together for God at the heart of Africa. CMS mission partners, alongside locally funded Christians, are involved in education and health care, such as that found in Gahini hospital in Rwanda, where ongoing projects include a feeding centre for malnourished babies as well as community health work and outreach. There is also a programme to help groups of orphans and widows. In Burundi there are support schemes for Bible school students who are being trained to be the future leaders of the church in mid-Africa.

Crafting the cross

A craft idea for making a similar cross

The cross of Rwanda and Burundi is a place of reconciliation, where traditional enemies might become brothers and sisters in Jesus.

Using the picture on page 28 as a guide, why not make a version of this cross for display, made up of as many different sorts of contrasting materials as possible? For example, you could include clay and stone, pieces of wood and fabric, metal and organic materials, paper and plastic.

Another approach might be to make a collage cross, deliberately choosing pictures of people who represent different extremes in colour, height, facial characteristics, ethnicity and age. The verse from Galatians referred to earlier could become the level ground on which this cross rests: 'All of you are God's children because of your faith in Christ Jesus' (Galatians 3:26).

An African crucifix

Bible link: Colossians 2:13b–15

God let Christ make you alive, when he forgave all our sins. God wiped out the charges that were against us for disobeying the Law of Moses. He took them away and nailed them to the cross. There Christ defeated all powers and forces. He let the whole world see them being led away as prisoners when he celebrated his victory.

Paul describes the cross as the place where debts are cancelled and the enemy is disarmed. It is evil that is being defeated on the cross, not Jesus.

Wondering about this Bible story

- I wonder how a death can make people alive?
- I wonder what the charges were that Paul says were against us?
- I wonder how we can be involved with defeating evil?

The story of this cross

This crucifix comes from Sierra Leone. It presents a mixture of styles and traditions. The idea of depicting a black Jesus on a cross is a comparatively recent one, whereas the little figures watching over his death come from a pre-Christian period in that country. They are ancient spirits who brought good luck and blessing to the crops or the family. Known as 'Nomolis', they are usually made of brass. Nomolis are part of traditional Mende history and culture (Mende is a tribal grouping of Sierra Leone).

Most representations of the person of Jesus show him as a white man, and there are few public exceptions to this, even in Sierra Leone. Only the east window of Christ the King, Freetown, a church that dates from the 1950s, has a black Jesus. This cross showing a black Christ being watched over by the Nomolis, who belong to the beliefs of the past, is therefore a modern version of a crucifix which has been earthed in traditional African culture.

The Nomolis have their hands folded across their chests, which is the traditional attitude of grief observed by the people of Sierra Leone. The Nomolis are reminiscent of the strange gargoyles and mythical creatures that are found on churches in Britain and which also accompany depictions of Jesus in early Celtic artwork. Perhaps the artist is expressing his or her belief that all of creation, past and present, mythical and human, pre- and post-Christian, stands in silent awe and grief before the death of Christ, which is the single most important event in all history.

Crafting the cross

A craft idea for making a similar cross

Working with a collection of multi-cultural images of Jesus, set up a small exhibition about the life of Jesus, with a particular focus on the cross. CMS, United Society for the Propagation of the Gospel (USPG) and the Methodist Church have published such a set of images under the title *The Christ We Share* (see contact details for CMS in the Appendix on page 156).

Explore what reactions visitors (such as other classes, different children's groups or adults from the church) have to these images. For example, is it important that there are pictures of a black Christ in such a collection?

Is it possible to design a crucifix that combines elements of all races and cultures? How could this be done?

A Lebanese cross

Bible link: Matthew 15:21–28

Jesus left and went to the territory near the cities of Tyre and Sidon. Suddenly a Canaanite woman from there came out shouting, 'Lord and Son of David, have pity on me! My daughter is full of demons.' Jesus did not say a word. But the woman kept following along and shouting, so his disciples came up and asked him to send her away. Jesus said, 'I was sent only to the people of Israel! They are like a flock of lost sheep.' The woman came closer. Then she knelt down and begged, 'Please help me, Lord!' Jesus replied, 'It isn't right to take food away from children and feed it to dogs.' 'Lord, that's true,' the woman said, 'but even dogs get the crumbs that fall from their owner's table.' Jesus answered, 'Dear woman, you really do have a lot of faith, and you will be given what you want.' At that moment her daughter was healed.

Jesus was in the area which is now modern Lebanon when he met a local woman who wanted her daughter to be healed. This story records how Jesus found extraordinary faith from a surprising person and in an unexpected place.

Wondering about this Bible story

• I wonder how the woman had heard about Jesus?
• I wonder why Jesus was so reluctant at first to answer her request?
• I wonder why Jesus was surprised by her words and her faith?

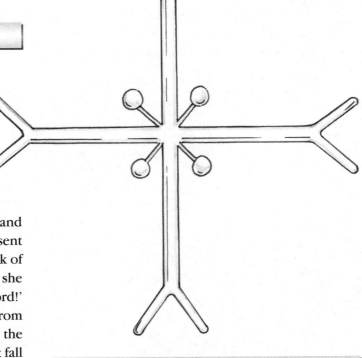

The story of this cross

This fifth-century Byzantine cross was discovered during the rebuilding of a monastery on an ancient site in the mountains of north Lebanon. It was carved into the stone and has now become the adopted symbol for the restored and redecorated Greek Orthodox monastery dedicated to St John the Baptist at Douma, near the village of Beit Chala. In recent years, Orthodox communities in this part of Lebanon have experienced a revival of spiritual life.

In the 1940s, two young theological students, George Hudud (who became the Greek Orthodox Bishop of Mount Lebanon) and his friend (who became Father Ephraim of St George's monastery near Beirut) began the *Mouvement de Jeunesse Orthodoxe*. Its leaders today are young adults concerned to deepen their faith in God and to work for a renewal of Orthodox spirituality and service in the lives of ordinary believers. They give their time to study and prayer as well as to leading camps for children and young people.

For the Orthodox believer, monasteries play an important role and become centres for regular retreats and pilgrimages, providing opportunities to seek spiritual counsel from the monks themselves. Following the disastrous years of civil war in Lebanon, there is now peace, and this has given an opportunity to rebuild and restore previously abandoned monastic sites. Many of these were themselves built over the foundations of very ancient churches, and some are high up on the mountainsides, accessible only on foot. Some of the restored buildings have even been reconstructed around very early cave churches dating from the first centuries of the Christian era.

The monastery of St John the Baptist, with its distinctive 'Lebanese cross', is being re-ordered and rebuilt as the result of the energy and vision of its Mother Superior, Mother Maria. Mother Maria herself was inspired by the frescoes at the Greek Orthodox monastery near Colchester, Essex, in the UK, where she took her vows as a nun under the Greek Orthodox Father Sophrony.

Greek Orthodox worship finds inspiration in a powerful and poetic liturgy, which is both sung and said, as well as beautiful frescoes and icons that cover every inch of the walls of the churches. Prayer is at the heart of its spiritual life and, in addition to attendance at the liturgy and the veneration of icons, special prayer ropes are popular. These ropes have a series of knots, rounded off with a bead and a simple knot in the shape of a cross. Each knot is fingered to accompany a repeated prayer—for example, the 'Jesus Prayer' (Lord Jesus Christ, Son of God, have mercy on me, a sinner)—as the worshipper stills herself or himself before God.

Crafting the cross

A craft idea for making a similar cross

Make your own version of the Lebanese cross by working it in either clay or Plasticine on a flat surface.

- What do you think the arrowheads on the arms of the crosses stand for?
- What do the circles mean?
- If you were designing a new cross for a new monastery or perhaps for your school or church group, what pattern would you create?

A craft idea for making a prayer rope

Using some coloured thin rope or thick string, tie a series of knots to create your own prayer rope as in the picture below. There are usually 33 knots in the circle. If you multiply this by three and add the final cross knot at the bottom, it comes to 100 repetitions of a given prayer.

The cross knot is made separately by sewing together four small knots and attaching them to the original circle of 33 knots through a small open bead.

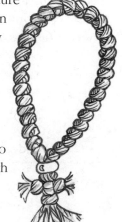

A palm cross

Bible link: John 12:12–15

The next day a large crowd was in Jerusalem for Passover. When they heard that Jesus was coming for the festival, they took palm branches and went out to greet him. They shouted, 'Hooray! God bless the one who comes in the name of the Lord! God bless the King of Israel!' Jesus found a donkey and rode on it, just as the Scriptures say, 'People of Jerusalem, don't be afraid! Your King is now coming, and he is riding on a donkey.'

Jesus was welcomed into Jerusalem by palm-waving crowds on the first Palm Sunday.

Wondering about this Bible story

- I wonder why Jesus chose to ride into the city on a young donkey?
- I wonder what Jesus was thinking about as he rode through the crowds?
- I wonder what the crowds expected to happen next?

The story of this cross

On Palm Sunday, many churches distribute crosses made from dried palm tree leaves to members of their congregations. The palm crosses help to remind people of the events of Holy Week that are about to be celebrated, culminating in Jesus' death on the cross on Good Friday and the resurrection from the empty tomb on Easter Sunday. They also recall the welcome that Jesus received as he rode into Jerusalem on a donkey, when people took branches from palm trees and went out to greet him, shouting, 'Hooray! God bless the one who comes in the name of the Lord!' (John 12:13).

The palm tree is very distinctive, with its tall, smooth trunk reaching high into the sky and its huge, fan-shaped leaves. Various species of palm tree are grown in many places in the tropics, and every part of the tree is used in some way. The following list includes some of the products that derive from the palm tree: sugar, wine, soap, brushes, hats, candles, mats, milk, timber, baskets, polish, edible buds and dates.

In some ways this great variety of end products or 'fruit' provides an interesting analogy for the fruit of the cross in the lives of Christians and the history of the world.

Crafting the cross

A craft idea for making a similar cross

For Palm Sunday, some churches buy crosses made in the Holy Land or Africa, but you could encourage your group to make their own 'palm' crosses. The simplest material to use is paper.

- Cut off strips from the long side of an A4 sheet, each strip to measure about 2cm wide.
- Join two strips together with sticky tape and taper one end, as illustrated below. Fold this long strip as outlined in the diagram.

- Depending on the size of the finished cross, you may need to use three strips joined together.
- As an alternative to paper, you may find other materials that you can use—ideally, some tough strips of long leaves, which would be a European equivalent of palm leaves.

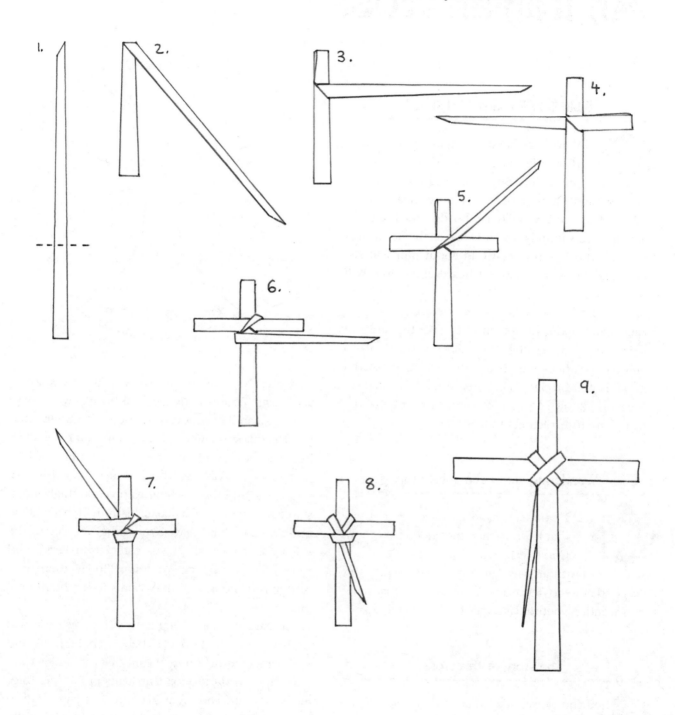

An Iranian cross

I have preached the good news about [Christ Jesus] all the way from Jerusalem to Illyricum. But I have always tried to preach where people have never heard about Christ. I am like a builder who doesn't build on anyone else's foundation. It is just as the Scriptures say, 'All who haven't been told about him will see him, and those who haven't heard about him will understand.'

Paul writes about his ambition to take the story of Jesus—the story of the cross and resurrection—to new parts of the world. He and the other apostles did just this and brought the Christian faith to most of the world known at the time within 100 years of the death and resurrection of Christ.

Wondering about this Bible story

- I wonder what Paul means by writing that he 'preached the good news about Christ Jesus'?
- I wonder why Paul was so keen to take this good news to new places in his world at that time?
- I wonder whether Paul ever felt like giving up?

The story of this cross

The present-day state of Iran used to be called Persia and as such has a long and distinguished history. In Old Testament times, the Persian empire ruled much of the Middle East under kings such as Darius. Darius even extended his rule into Europe. Persian manners, good taste, etiquette and tradition were well respected.

An early religion of the Persians was Zoroastrianism. Zoroastra himself was born in what today is Azerbaijan. He believed in one God and an afterlife. His followers did not believe in statues or altars but burned sacrificial fires on mountaintops as part of their worship. The Avesta is their book of scriptures, and their teachings promote high moral standards, with a particular hatred of lying. One tradition says that the wise men who were led by the star to find the baby Jesus came from Persia and were of this religious tradition. Today there is a recognized site in Iran that claims to be their burial place.

Christianity was brought to Persia by Nestorian Christians. Their particular beliefs about Jesus and their views on the Trinity meant that often they were persecuted by Orthodox Christians in Europe. Later in the seventh and eighth centuries, Islam came to Persia, and today it remains the dominant faith of the country. Muslims in modern-day Iran belong to the Shiite tradition and are strongly influenced by Sufi mysticism—an aspect of Islamic belief that stresses the need for prayer and meditation. Some of Iran's greatest thinkers and poets, such as Hafiz and Saadi, were influenced by Sufi thinking.

In Iran today, officially there is religious freedom. At times in recent history, however, Christianity and other non-Muslim faiths have suffered suppression. All people of whatever faith are required to observe Islamic codes of public conduct. Other faith groups are represented in Parliament (the Majlis), and their religious buildings are open.

According to government sources, there are over 176 churches, 21 synagogues and 36 temples in Iran. The largest concentration of Christian churches is in West Azerbaijan, and most Christians are of the Armenian and Assyrian tradition. There is a small Anglican community in the capital Tehran.

The cross in this resource is that adopted by the 'Friends of the Anglican Diocese of Iran', which was established in 1912.

Near the village of Qareh Kandy, in western Iran, is the world-famous St Tadeos Church, which is a place of pilgrimage for Armenian Christians from all around the globe. In July, many hundreds of pilgrims join in with a special service, which often includes baptisms and weddings. The church itself is very impressive, made from black basalt stone and contrasting engraved white stones. Often it is called *Qareh Kelissa*, which means 'the black church'. St Tadeos was a first-century martyr for the Christian faith, and it is traditionally believed that he is buried here. He brought Christianity to the area and succeeded in converting the king's daughter. In anger, King Sanardrok had both the saint and his own daughter put to death. It is claimed that she was the first female Christian martyr.

Crafting the cross

A craft idea for making a similar cross

A version of this cross could be painted in blacks and whites, to connect with the appearance of St Tadeos Church; for the more adventurous, an embroidered version of the cross could perhaps be attempted in the manner of the famous patterns on Persian carpets.

The Jerusalem cross

Bible link: Revelation 7:9–10

After this, I saw a large crowd with more people than could be counted. They were from every race, tribe, nation, and language, and they stood before the throne and before the Lamb. They wore white robes and held palm branches in their hands, as they shouted, 'Our God, who sits upon the throne, has the power to save his people, and so does the Lamb.'

John's vision of the Church at the end of time is of a massive international and cross-cultural family drawn from the four corners of the world. Their one focus is 'the Lamb', which was the way the first Christians described Jesus who had died on the cross for all.

Wondering about this Bible story

- I wonder whether differences of culture, class and colour will still matter in heaven?
- I wonder what really can unite all Christians?
- I wonder how Christians today can best demonstrate that they are part of such a global and multi-cultural church?

The story of this cross

This distinctive Christian cross comes from the very part of the world where the Christian story first began. It is used today by the church in that part of the Middle East, where there is a significant Palestinian Christian minority, which has maintained the faith and has roots that go right back to biblical times. For example, the Anglican Diocese of Jerusalem uses this cross as a focus of unity for its widely scattered congregations in Jordan, Lebanon, Syria, Egypt, Iran, Libya, Tunisia, Algeria, Cyprus and Ethiopia.

There are two variations of the usual form of this cross. The first (known as the cross crosslet) is one in which four Latin crosses, each of which represents a point of the compass, are joined together. The second (called St Julian's cross) takes a form in which the four Latin crosses are set diagonally to each other.

The Jerusalem cross has also been adopted in other parts of the world, particularly as a symbol for ecumenical gatherings of believers, such as the bi-annual *Kirchentag* in Germany, at which the Protestant churches come together for four days of interaction, talks, musical events, Bible readings and a huge resources exhibition.

One interpretation of the Jerusalem cross, which is in fact a combination of five crosses, is that it is a visual representation of the growth of the Christian Church, extending out into the world, just as Jesus had commanded when he commissioned his first disciples just before his ascension. The main and largest cross is centred on Jerusalem where this growth of the Church began. The other four crosses, located in the spaces between the crosspiece and the upright, represent the Church today, visible in the four corners of the earth.

A craft idea for making a similar cross

The craft idea for this cross picks up this theme of the worldwide Church.

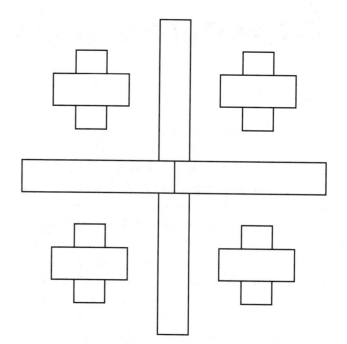

- Colour in the land and the sea (green and blue respectively) on a photocopy of the map of the world below.
- Cut the map of the world up into eight equal strips.
- Use four of the strips to make up the central cross with its equal arms.
- Cut each of the remaining four strips in half. These eight halves form the four other crosses that go into the spaces between the crosspieces and the uprights of the largest cross.
- Stick all the pieces on to a piece of card as a representation of the Jerusalem cross, illustrating how the good news of Jesus Christ has gone out, 'starting from Jerusalem', into all the world.

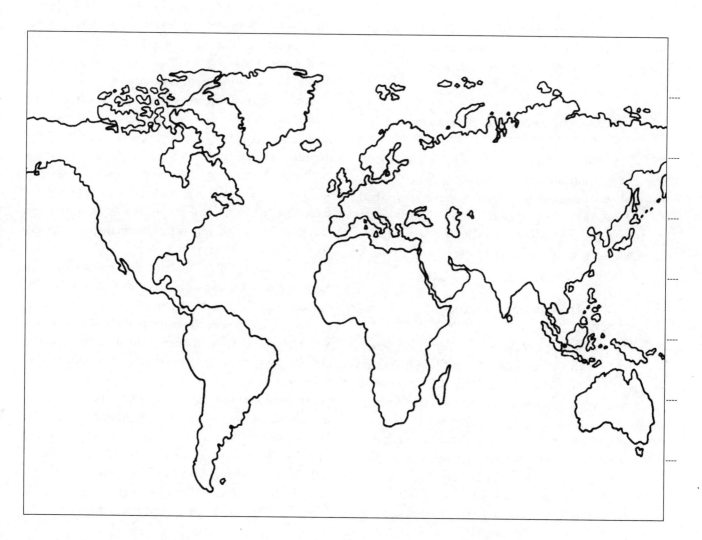

Reproduced with permission from *A–Cross the World* published by BRF 2004 (1 84101 264 5)

St Andrew's cross

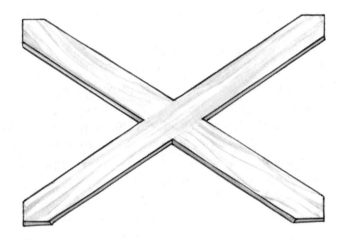

Bible link: John 1:40–42

One of the two men who had heard John [the Baptist] and had gone with Jesus was Andrew, the brother of Simon Peter. The first thing Andrew did was to find his brother and tell him, 'We have found the Messiah!' The Hebrew word 'Messiah' means the same as the Greek word 'Christ'. Andrew brought his brother to Jesus. And when Jesus saw him, he said, 'Simon son of John, you will be called Cephas.' This name can be translated as 'Peter' [which means 'rock'].

John the Baptist encouraged his disciples to follow Jesus. The news spread, and Andrew found his brother and brought him to join the others.

Wondering about this Bible story

- I wonder how Andrew felt about introducing his brother to Jesus?
- I wonder how Andrew was so sure that Jesus was the person God had promised to send?
- I wonder how Andrew felt when he heard Jesus speak such special words to Peter?

The story of this cross

St Andrew has long been associated with the mission of the Church. Those incidents in the Gospel that directly involve him reveal a man who was interested in passing on the good news and, in particular, reaching out to outsiders. Once he had left the fishing industry to follow Jesus, he was quick to bring along his brother to join the growing band of disciples. Later, it was Andrew who introduced some Greeks to Jesus, and it was also Andrew who recognized that a child's picnic might be something special in the hands of Jesus. It is chiefly because of his first recorded words ('We have found the Messiah', John 1:41) that Andrew is known not only as the 'first called' (the 'protoclete' in Greek) but also the first missionary.

Little is known of Andrew's missionary career after Pentecost, though various traditions agree that he travelled in Asia Minor (present-day Turkey), along the Black Sea and as far as the River Volga. Countries in Eastern Europe lay claim to Andrew's missionary activities, and Russia has adopted him as a patron saint. He died in Greece at Patras, traditionally crucified like Jesus but on a distinctive 'X'-shaped cross (a saltire cross).

St Andrew's link to Scotland arises from another tradition, which claims that his relics were taken by monks from Byzantium (Istanbul), who were setting out to take the gospel to Scotland in the sixth century AD. Where they buried these remains they built a church, and today this site is in the city known as St Andrews.

Andrew certainly seems to have been a great traveller and, ever since 1871, St Andrew's Day (30 November) has been a special time of prayer for world mission. It was in this year that another 'modern' missionary figure, Bishop John Patterson, was martyred in Melanesia. The following is a St Andrew's Day prayer from the New Zealand prayer book:

Everliving God,
Your apostle Andrew obeyed the call of your Son,
And followed him without delay;
Grant that we like him may give ourselves readily
To do what you command; through our Saviour
Jesus Christ.
Jesus, when you call
May we like Andrew leave our nets,
our home, our everything, to follow you.

Crafting the cross

A craft idea for making a similar cross

St Andrew is often depicted with the symbol of a fishing net. This represents both his original trade and his new work for Jesus as 'a fisher for people'.

Why not use some simple plastic netting from a garden shop and create the shape of the St Andrew's cross? The cross is usually white (for purity) on a blue background (representing the seas over which he carried the gospel and the sea of Galilee where he worked). The netting could be painted or coloured appropriately. Individual fish symbols could be attached in between the arms of the cross, each carrying words or pictures but illustrating different incidents from the life of Andrew (for example, the calling of his brother, his help at the feeding of the five thousand, meeting Jesus and following him, and introducing the Greeks to Jesus).

Alternatively, each 'fish' could represent the different ways in which Christians try to follow Andrew's example by taking the love of God out to those in need and those who have not yet heard of Jesus.

The diagonal 'X'-shaped cross could also be the centrepiece for a display on God's mission work today in the very places where Andrew or his relics are reputed to have gone, namely Greece, Russia (or another eastern European country), Turkey and Scotland. Each arm of the cross becomes an arrow pointing to what is happening in those places today. For information on the different countries, contact CMS (see details in the Appendix on page 156).

A South Indian cross

Bible link: John 17:20–21

I am not praying just for these followers. I am also praying for everyone else who will have faith because of what my followers will say about me. I want all of them to be one with each other, just as I am one with you and you are one with me. I also want them to be one with us. Then the people of this world will believe that you sent me.

This is the last part of Jesus' final prayer before he was arrested in the garden of Gethsemane, as recorded in John's Gospel.

Wondering about this Bible story

- I wonder why Jesus thought it was important to pray this prayer?
- I wonder how and when this prayer is answered?
- I wonder how you would like this prayer to be answered?

The story of this cross

In 1997, the Church of South India celebrated its golden jubilee. In 1947 a united church was formed by bringing together most Protestant denominations in one body, so that they might provide a collective expression of the message of Jesus Christ to the people of south India.

This united church has adopted a very distinctive cross as one of its symbols. The basic cross is red and represents Jesus' death for the forgiveness of sins. Superimposed on the cross in this design is the lotus flower. This is a cultural image that denotes the holiness of God. The lotus grows out of the mud and, in a similar way, our lives, though surrounded by the mud of all that spoils our world, can blossom into something beautiful because of Jesus' sacrifice. The lotus is an eastern symbol of God's closeness. In the design it is saffron in colour.

Around this cross are set words from John 17:21, part of Jesus' prayer that his followers would 'be one'. This unity is to be a witness to the world that Jesus was sent by God and that what he says is true. In many ways the Church of South India has set the Christian world an example of obedience to this prayer, which has been an important factor in its growing life and witness.

Tradition holds that St Thomas the apostle brought the faith to India in AD52. By the year 200, the Orthodox Church was established in south-west India. Records indicate that a bishop was sent from Jerusalem to India in 345, and in 530 a traveller reported the existence of Christian communities both in south-west India and Sri Lanka.

It is said that Thomas crossed the Red Sea and then the Persian Gulf to the port of Cranganore in Kerala on the Malabar coast. The 'Malabar Christians' or 'Thomas Christians' were well established by the year 200. They were linked for many centuries to the Nestorian church in Mesopotamia through the Patriarch of Baghdad. (It is recorded that the Patriarch of Baghdad sent bishops to Malabar in 1490.) In 1599, however, they renounced Nestorianism—a doctrine that attributed to Christ two separate persons, one human and the other divine—and allied themselves with Rome.

This branch of the Malabar Christians eventually became known as the Malankara Orthodox Syrian Church. In 1653, some of the Malabar Christians opted for independence from Rome and seceded with their own bishop. In 1816, CMS sent four missionaries to help this independent church by teaching at its seminary and helping in the translation of the scriptures. CMS established a theological college at Kottayam.

In 1829, the impetus of a reform movement within the church led to divisions that resulted in the formation of the Mar Thoma Syrian Church of Malabar or, as it's more popularly known, the Mar Thoma Church. The churches of north and south India and the Mar Thoma Church have entered into a conciliar union that brings together traditions of Christianity from both east and west.

Another cross that is commonly seen in India is known as the St Thomas cross or the 'Anuradhapuram', which is often worn on a long pendant around the neck.

Crafting the cross

A craft idea for making a similar cross

Enlarge the template of this cross and use it to create your own variation of the design. Start by colouring the basic cross a bright red. For this you could use paprika, which is a red pepper from India. Cover the surface of the cross with glue from a glue stick. Sprinkle the paprika over the drawing and then shake off the excess. Repeat this exercise until enough of the paprika has stuck to the shape of the cross to make it a clear red.

Cut some yellow tissue paper into strips of different lengths and widths. Curl these strips into the shapes of leaves, which should then be stuck on to the cross, following the outlines of the lotus leaves on the original illustration.

If you choose to add the motto (part of the verse from John's Gospel), you may like to use letters of the alphabet from different magazines and in different colours to illustrate the variety and unity of the church, which is reflected by this message.

THAT THEY ALL MAY BE ONE

CHURCH OF SOUTH INDIA

Reproduced with permission from A–Cross the World published by BRF 2004 (1 84101 264 5)

A North Indian cross

Bible link: Mark 14:22–23

During the meal Jesus took some bread in his hands. He blessed the bread and broke it. He gave it to his disciples and said, 'Take this. It is my body.' Jesus picked up a cup of wine and gave thanks to God. He gave it to his disciples, and said, 'Drink it!' So they all drank some.

At the last meal before his crucifixion, Jesus gave his followers a simple way of remembering all that he had taught them. The bread and the wine, which they shared, were symbols that showed how he was giving himself up out of love for them.

Wondering about this Bible story

• I wonder if the disciples really understood what Jesus was trying to say that night?

• I wonder what the bread and wine say about unity, witness and service?

• I wonder what the bread and wine really mean to Christians?

The story of this cross

The Church Mission Society (CMS) began its work in India in 1813. The first Anglican ordination of an Indian, Abdul Masih, occurred in 1825. Abdul Masih had worked with the great missionary Henry Martyn, whose translation of the Gospel into Urdu, Persian and partly into Arabic left a lasting legacy for future Christian work in the Indian subcontinent. In particular, missionaries advanced the education of girls and women and pioneered work with people who were blind or deaf. In many instances CMS shared its work with the Church of England Zenana Missionary Society (CEZMS), which also took a particular interest in work among women. The CEZMS merged with CMS in 1957.

In the early 1920s, a delegation of CMS directors reported a need to transfer control of the mission in India from CMS to the local church. The Anglican Church in India achieved its independence, as a self-governing 'province' within the worldwide Anglican Church, in 1930.

The Church of North India (CNI) was formed in 1970, uniting most of the Protestant denominations in the north, in similar fashion to the Church of South India. The church runs a large number of educational institutions and has a special concern for the poorest people in Indian society.

The logo for the CNI is a golden cross on a red background. The centre of the cross is surrounded by the petals of a flower that border a red circle, which in turn contains a communion cup or chalice. The key words of the CNI's motto are inscribed around the logo, namely Unity, Witness and Service. The CNI's united witness is most clearly demonstrated in the way the church pours itself out for those who are marginalized in any way by society, in the same way as Jesus poured out his life, symbolized by the wine poured and drunk at holy communion.

Here is an Easter prayer from north India:

Almighty God, eternally we praise you for raising Jesus our Lord from the dead on Easter Day. We praise you for resurrecting also the life of his first disciples, empowering them to carry your mission throughout the world. Risen Lord, resurrect once again your Church, that it may follow you in liberating all people from the power of sin and suffering, and in establishing justice and peace throughout the world. Amen.

Crafting the cross

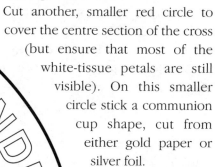

A craft idea for making a similar cross

You will need red card, white tissue paper and gold paper or silver foil.

The cross has five layers and, like the various denominational groups that have come together in the CNI, the layers interact with and rely on each other to build up a united witness to the gospel.

- First of all, cut a circle of red card as the background to the cross.
- Using the white tissue paper, create an eight-petalled flower that you can attach to the centre of the red circle.
- Next, cut out a card cross according to the pattern in the picture below and cover the cross with gold paper. This cross should be placed over the flower on the red background.
- Cut another, smaller red circle to cover the centre section of the cross (but ensure that most of the white-tissue petals are still visible). On this smaller circle stick a communion cup shape, cut from either gold paper or silver foil.
- Finally, use a black marker pen to draw around the inner circle where it borders the flower, to make the communion cup stand out.

A Bangladeshi cross

Bible link: James 2:1–5

My friends, if you have faith in our glorious Lord Jesus Christ, you won't treat some people better than others. Suppose a rich person wearing fine clothes and a gold ring comes to one of your meetings. And suppose a poor person dressed in worn-out clothes also comes. You must not give the best seat to the one in fine clothes and tell the one who is poor to stand at the side or sit on the floor. That is the same as saying that some people are better than others, and you would be acting like a crooked judge. My dear friends, pay attention. God has given a lot of faith to the poor people in this world. He has also promised them a share in his kingdom that he will give to everyone who loves him.

James challenged his readers about their un-Christlike attitude to those who were not wealthy and powerful. It is so often the poor in the world who are more clear-sighted about what really matters and who can teach others about true faith.

Wondering about this Bible story

- I wonder whether the Church is as much caught in favouritism to the rich today as it was in James' time?
- I wonder why people are so frightened of listening to the poor?
- I wonder what it is that the poor can teach us about faith?

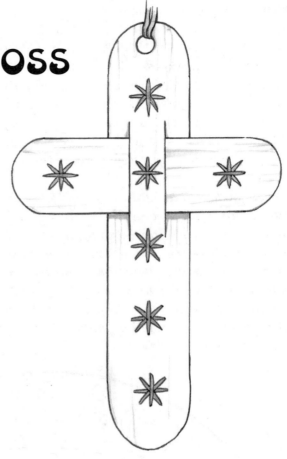

The story of this cross

Mrs Bitihika Baroi is a member of her local Church of Bangladesh congregation in Jobarpur, southern Bangladesh. She is also the women's group leader in Shorbari village.

She had the original idea to generate income by using the leaves of the bamboo trees, which grow everywhere in the region, to make bamboo crosses. With some advice from her husband, she also devised the process of cutting the leaves into strips, boiling and drying them, using an iron cutting mould to cut out the two axes of the cross, then interlocking them and sewing on coloured thread.

About 40 crosses can be made from one leaf, and a woman making around 30 in a day will earn 2.5 taka per cross.

A group in the nearby village of Aksor also took up making the crosses. Mrs Suchitra Shigde, a Christian who leads this group of mainly Hindu women, said, 'At first our husbands ridiculed us for spending part of the day making these crosses while they were hard at work in the fields. Then, when they saw that we were able to sell them and that they were going abroad, their attitude changed. Our husbands now give us more respect.'

The women also understand something of the meaning of the cross as revealing God's love in Christ, so they realize that their work has a special value. These women's groups are part of the NOK women's empowerment programme of the Church of Bangladesh.

This project is based around three villages in the Barisal district of the country and is called NOK from the initials of three villages—Narikelbari, Oichermath, Kandi. The crosses are sold as part of a credit- and income-generating scheme. Many such schemes have been set up by the church. They target landless labourers, small and marginal farmers, malnourished mothers, widows and poor families. Sadly, present high interest rates create a seemingly unavoidable trap of debt-dependency for these groups.

A typical scheme begins with a savings group run by local women. The amount saved creates a fund from which interest-free loans can be taken in rotation. Each woman or family then puts what is borrowed into projects such as the cultivation of a piece of land, opening a small shop or starting the production of craft items. The aim is to transform lives by making independence a truly achievable goal. Alongside these schemes, the church has encouraged the growth of small literacy programmes. The vision of the Church of Bangladesh is to find ways to share and show God's love and help people to express and experience the fullness of life that Jesus promised.

The cross in the illustration is made from bamboo leaves and has been embroidered with coloured cotton stars.

Crafting the cross

A craft idea for making a similar cross

To make your own version of this cross, you could use card and coloured stars. Use the picture to create a template. Make two parallel cuts about two-thirds of the way up the vertical piece of the cross, through which you can thread the horizontal crosspiece.

Alternatively, it would be appropriate to make the cross from paper, since in Bangladesh scrap paper is used to make paper bags, which are sold by children to earn a little money.

A Pakistani cross

Bible link: 1 Corinthians 1:23–27

We preach that Christ was nailed to a cross. Most Jews have problems with this, and most Gentiles think it is foolish. Our message is God's power and wisdom for the Jews and the Greeks that he has chosen. Even when God is foolish, he is wiser than everyone else, and even when God is weak, he is stronger than everyone else. My dear friends, remember what you were when God chose you. The people of this world didn't think that many of you were wise. Only a few of you were in places of power, and not many of you came from important families. But God chose the foolish things of this world to put the wise to shame. He chose the weak things of this world to put the powerful to shame.

The apostle Paul wrote to the Christians in Corinth, who were for the most part some of the poorest and least powerful of that city's citizens. He acknowledged that many people see the cross as a foolish way for God to choose to rescue the world.

Wondering about this Bible story

- I wonder why God so often chooses the least and the last in the world's eyes?
- I wonder why people at the time Paul was writing found the message of the cross so strange and foolish?
- I wonder whether people today still find the cross a foolish way to change the world?

The story of this cross

The Church of Pakistan has adopted as its symbol an ancient design of a cross that was found at an archeological site near Islamabad. It dates from the fifth century and, as such, predates the dominant Islamic presence in modern Pakistan, reminding the church that the Christian faith arrived there in the first centuries of the Christian era and that Pakistani Christians today follow in the footsteps of a long line of people from that part of the world who have been disciples of Jesus Christ.

In 1995, this Taxila cross was particularly used to celebrate the 25th anniversary of the united Christian Church of Pakistan. This church is often under pressure in a largely Muslim society, and the existence for Christians of their own particular national cross is an encouragement to pass on the faith despite the hardships that they often encounter. A well-known chorus used by Pakistani Christians sums up this challenge and takes the form of a prayer that they might remain firm in what they believe:

Yisu ke pichhe main chalne laga, na lautunga, na lautunga…

'I have begun to follow Jesus, no turning back, no turning back…'

A craft idea for making a similar cross

In Pakistan, Christians often come from the poorer classes of Pakistani society and live in *bustees* (slums). They work as rubbish clearers and road sweepers.

As a prayerful reminder of this fact, why not collect together some 'clean' rubbish such as sweet wrappers and food packets in appropriate colours and use them to make a collage on an enlarged photocopy of the template of the Taxila cross.

The striped area should be predominantly red and the rest a white or cream colour. Photocopy the template below on to some thin card so that you have a firm foundation for the coloured wrappings.

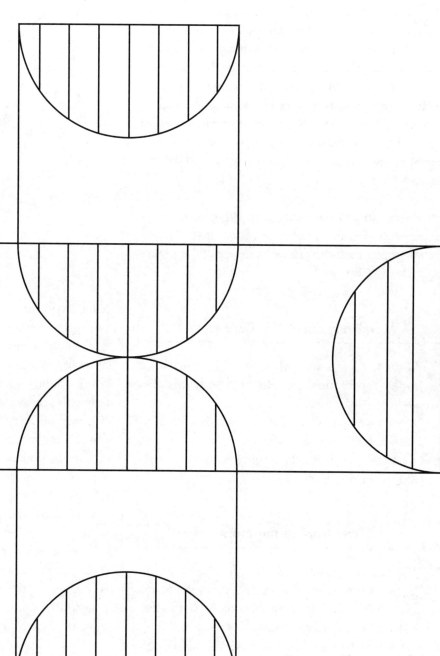

A Georgian cross

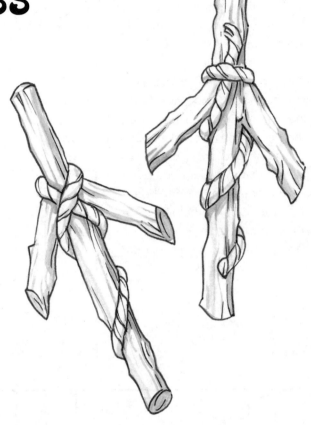

Bible link: 2 Kings 5:1–3

Naaman was the commander of the Syrian army. The Lord had helped him and his troops defeat their enemies, so the king of Syria respected Namaan very much. Namaan was a brave soldier, but he had leprosy. One day while the Syrian troops were raiding Israel, they captured a girl, and she became a servant of Namaan's wife. Some time later the girl said, 'If your husband Namaan would go to the prophet in Samaria, he would be cured of his leprosy.'

This is the story of the young slave girl who, like Nina in the story you are about to read, was instrumental in bringing her master to an experience of the power of the living God.

Wondering about this Bible story

- I wonder whether the voices of powerless people can really make a difference?
- I wonder why Naaman's wife bothered to listen to her slave girl's advice?
- I wonder how the maid managed to go on trusting God in her situation?

The story of this cross

In the capital of Georgia, part of the Commonwealth of Independent States (CIS), at the Orthodox Sioni Cathedral, there is a historic cross known as St Nina's cross, which is unique to the Christians of this ancient country.

The story behind it concerns a Christian slave-girl,

Nina, who had been captured and brought to Georgia to serve at the court of King Mirian. Through her simple witness she was able to share the good news of Jesus with the king. Later, around AD330, the whole country adopted Christianity. As a visual aid for telling the gospel story, Nina brought with her a cross that was, in fact, part of a branch from a vine bush. It was distinctive in that each end of the horizontal crosspiece pointed downwards. In this form it is seen as a cross of submission, symbolizing both the humility of Christ and the humble origins of Nina who brought the Christian faith to this part of the world.

A rope is wound around the cross, and this is a reminder of the way in which Jesus' followers are to be 'slaves' in the service of others. It also reminds people that many of his followers paid the ultimate price of martyrdom.

Crafting the cross

A craft idea for making a similar cross

Making a version of St Nina's cross could be a simple craft activity for a group to undertake. It may be that you could find suitable twigs or parts of branches that would give you the appropriate cross shape, which could then be varnished and have a rope wound around its centre (see the drawings of the cross on page 50). If twigs or branches are not available, then the downward-pointing crosspieces would need to be attached with glue or masking tape, which could be disguised and strengthened by painting over the whole cross before varnishing it and winding the rope around its middle.

This activity could be introduced in collective worship or as part of a service by bringing in various differently shaped, fallen twigs or branches from a bush or tree. Ask the children what objects the shapes of the branches and twigs remind them of (possible suggestions might range from catapults to creatures of various kinds). Use this as a means of explaining how St Nina's vine branch reminded her of Jesus' cross and led to the beginning of the story of Christian faith in Georgia.

An Asian cross

Bible link: Matthew 13:45–46

Jesus continued: The kingdom of heaven is like what happens when a shop owner is looking for fine pearls. After finding a very valuable one, the owner goes and sells everything in order to buy that pearl.

Jesus told this parable of the shop owner in search of the finest pearl.

Wondering about this Bible story

- I wonder who would sell so valuable a pearl to this shop owner?
- I wonder how the shop owner felt once he had purchased the finest pearl?
- I wonder what this pearl really is and what it is really like to own it?

The story of this cross

The Christian faith has ancient roots in many parts of Asia, sometimes predating subsequent domination by other faiths and philosophies. This ancient cross combines symbols from Asian culture with the roots of the gospel and hopes for the future.

At each of the points of this cross is set a 'pearl'. The four 'pearls' represent the pearls of the Gospel story as told by the four Gospel writers. The teachings of Jesus are that pearl of great price for which it is worth sacrificing all else. Off the coasts of Asia, pearl-divers plunge into the depths of the sea to search for the most costly and beautiful pearls, which they extract from oyster shells. This practice itself provides an analogy for the continuous search for the truth about life and its value.

The cross is set within the lotus flower which, in Asian culture, is an enduring symbol of divine holiness. This flower, which grows in beauty out of the mud in which it is rooted, represents the spiritual dimension in all people that can grow out of, and transform, the ordinariness of our everyday lives.

In this design, rays of light spread out in every direction from the heart of the cross, reaching out and embracing all people. God's love for the world in Christ is an inclusive, generous love that touches everyone, whatever his or her traditions or beliefs. Christians believe that Jesus holds the key to awareness, true enlightenment and salvation for the whole world.

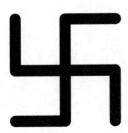

Another eastern cross that is originally from Asia and has an interesting cross-cultural history is the swastika. The name derives from the Sanskrit word for 'well-being', and it is a sign of prosperity and good fortune.

Examples of this cross occur in early Christian art, where it was known as the 'gammadion cross' because it could be created from four capital gammas. Gamma is the third letter of the Greek alphabet, Γ. Today, Buddhists, Hindus and Jains also use this cross symbol to depict the life force of the sun, which appears to move clockwise in the northern hemisphere.

A version of this symbol, with the arms revolving in the opposite direction, was adopted by the National Socialist movement in Germany and now has very negative associations for people in the West because of the atrocities committed in the name of the Nazi regime under Hitler.

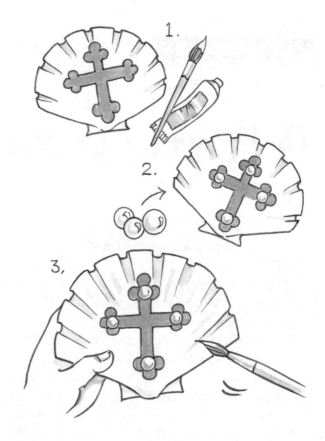

Crafting the cross

A craft idea for making a similar cross

A version of the first cross could be made using shells. Packs of shells are available from craft shops. However, your class or group may perhaps have collections at home, gathered on seaside holidays.

- Choose a scallop shell and paint or draw the basic cross design on to it.
- Glue on artificial pearls (also available from craft shops) at the four points of the cross.

- Create the effect of the lotus flower either by painting in rays on to the background of the shell or, on a larger scale, by selecting razor shells which should be painted yellow and arranged as rays around the edge of the scallop shell.
- Use other shells to decorate and complete the design.

A Korean cross

Leopards will lie down with young goats, and wolves will rest with lambs. Calves and lions will eat together and be cared for by little children. Cows and bears will share the same pasture; their young will rest side by side. Lions and oxen will both eat straw. Little children will play near snake holes. They will stick their hands into dens of poisonous snakes and never be hurt. Nothing harmful will take place on the Lord's holy mountain. Just as water fills the sea, the land will be filled with people who know and honour the Lord.

The prophet Isaiah foresaw the day when God's special king—the Messiah—would bring together all of creation to a place of peace and safety. Traditional enemies would become friends and the last and the least would be treated with fairness and honesty.

Wondering about this Bible story

- I wonder how Isaiah thought this vision would come about?
- I wonder what this has to do with Jesus and the cross?
- I wonder if there are any signs that this vision is becoming true today?

The story of this cross

The Holy Catholic Church (which is the name given to the Anglican Church in Korea) uses this cross as its nationally recognized symbol. John Corfe, the first Anglican bishop of Korea (inaugurated in 1889), was the person who initially introduced this style of cross to Korea. Korea became an independent Province of the Anglican Communion in 1993.

In Korean art, there are recognizable symbols that are used to convey the blessing of a long life. These include representations of turtles, pine trees (over three-quarters of Korea is mountainous and in recent years much of it has been successfully reforested), mountains, bamboo, water, the moon and flying cranes. However, by far the most powerful symbol of life is the sun. The Korean cross is designed to imitate the shape of this symbol but, at the same time, to point to Christ as the true source of eternal blessing.

Almost one-third of South Korea's population is Christian, and they place a great emphasis on fellowship and prayer. Churches are very large. Seoul, the capital, is home to the single largest church fellowship in the world (over 600,000 people!). Despite its technological advancement, there are nevertheless many internal challenges to life in Korea today. There are groups of poor and deprived people who are casualties of an affluent society. The Anglican Church in particular is involved with these groups through the work of the 'Houses of Sharing', which are small social-welfare centres set up to give people a voice and a place to meet and pray together.

A crucial issue in Korea for many Christians and

non-Christians alike is the continuing division of the nation after the Korean War which, officially, is still not over. Many in the south of the country are still separated from relatives whose homes are in the north, beyond the demilitarized zone. Christians pray and work for national reconciliation and an end to the political divide.

Crafting the cross

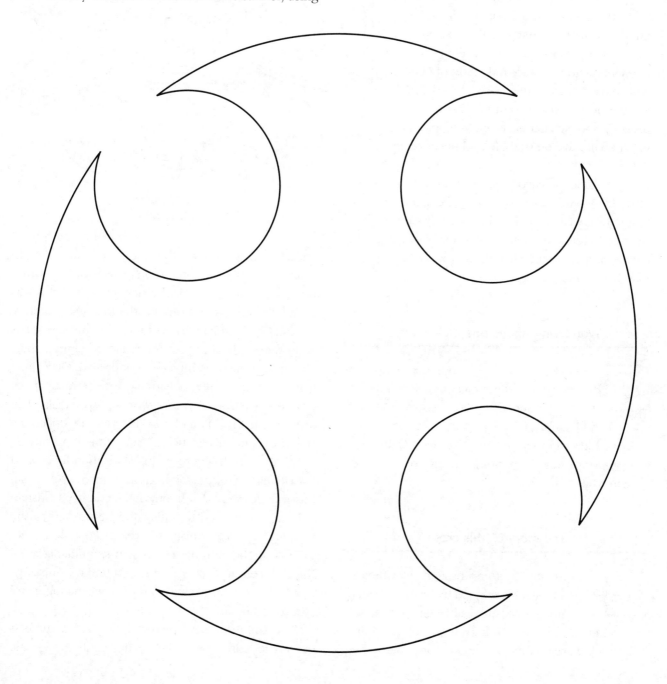

A craft idea for making a similar cross

The cross is usually depicted in red on a white background. One idea for a craft activity would be to make a fabric banner, using pieces of cloth in different colours to create or represent the key symbols of long life mentioned above. These could be arranged around a piece of red cloth, cut in the shape of the Korean cross.

A simpler approach would be to use fabric pens to draw the shape of the Korean cross on pieces of curtain-lining material. Maybe this material could then be cut in the geographical shape of Korea.

On the BRF website is a copy of a wall-hanging designed by You-n Koo Lee. It includes the cross and some other images to celebrate the partnership of the three Korean Anglican dioceses and CMS. This hanging is, in its turn, based on one that is found in one of the 'Houses of Sharing' in Seoul; the original is also on the BRF website.

Reproduced with permission from *A–Cross the World* published by BRF 2004 (1 84101 264 5)

A Chinese cross

Bible link: John 3:13–16

Jesus replied: No one has gone up to heaven except the Son of Man, who came down from there. And the Son of Man must be lifted up, just as that metal snake was lifted up by Moses in the desert. Then everyone who has faith in the Son of Man will have eternal life. God loved the people of this world so much that he gave his only Son, so that everyone who has faith in him will have eternal life and never really die.

Jesus explained to Nicodemus the mystery of the new birth he would have to experience if he were to follow Jesus. He also describes the cross (the 'lifting up') by reference to the story of Moses and the bronze serpent, which healed all who looked up at it (see Numbers 21:4–9).

Wondering about this Bible story

- I wonder why Nicodemus chose to come secretly at night to talk with Jesus?
- I wonder why Jesus spoke in such 'coded' language?
- I wonder whether the metal snake might be a confusing picture for some people of the cross and what it means?

The story of this cross

Christianity was first brought to China in AD635 in a mission led by Bishop Olopen. He came from Persia and belonged to the branch of the church known as the Nestorians. This group were very mission-minded and established

churches in India and other parts of central Asia. In China, the emperor at the time of the bishop's arrival had a cathedral built for the new faith, and this was soon followed by many other cathedrals and churches.

The Christian faith as presented by the Nestorians was open to local influences as far as traditional art and indigenous worship were concerned. Over time, Chinese Christianity began to absorb many local customs, such as ancestor worship (particularly of former emperors), and it was also influenced by Buddhist symbolism, such as that of the lotus flower.

In the ninth century AD, both Buddhists and Christians were persecuted and many Nestorian missionaries were driven out of the country. Christian believers continued to suffer and be pushed to the margins, especially during the years of the Mongolian invasions. The faith did not regain its influence until the 14th century when, as result of Catholic missions from the West, Christianity was once again taught and spread in China.

The Chinese cross pictured in this resource is from the early Nestorian years and shows the influence of local culture, including lotus flower shapes—patterns that relate to Buddhist ideas about the transmigration of souls—and also the 'gammadion' shape, which is used in the East as a symbol of well-being and happiness.

Recent archeological finds in China have unearthed Christian churches that were built over with Chinese pagodas. One, at Da Qin near Xian, the capital of Shaanxi province, contains stone slabs inscribed with stories about Jesus (Jesus Sutras). They also include a radical version of the Ten Commandments, which taught no violence to any living creature and thus promoted vegetarianism.

The Church in China has continued to go through periods of great growth and sudden persecution. At the beginning of the Communist years last century, the missionaries were once again expelled. Nevertheless, the Christian Church did continue to flourish, and today there are official state-recognized churches as well as many secret groups of believers. Some estimate that there could be as many as 50 million believers in Jesus in China today.

The first CMS missionaries went to China in 1844, and the first Chinese Anglican to be ordained was Dzaw Tsanglae in 1863. The Church in China calls itself a 'three-self' church, following principles first developed by CMS General Secretary Henry Venn (in the mid-19th century), namely that churches should be self-financing, self-governing and self-extending.

Some questions to consider:

- Do you think Christians should try to absorb aspects of local culture into their presentation of the gospel?
- In what ways do missionaries need to listen to what God is already doing in a culture and then bring alongside it their understanding of who Jesus is and how he may fulfil what the local people already know about God?
- The Nestorian Christians were happy to incorporate local art and traditional ideas into their presentation of the Christian faith. Do you think they were right? Can missionaries go too far in this? What are the boundaries?
- Look at the Chinese cross with its different indigenous elements. Does this help or hinder the presentation of the Christian faith in your view?
- If you were to create a cross using the spiritual aspirations and the cultural understandings about God that are prevalent in our society today, what would such a cross look like?

Crafting the cross

A craft idea for making a similar cross

Chinese literary 'seals' are usually a symmetrical combination of Chinese characters printed in red. You could make a seal using the shape of the Nestorian cross, either by carving the outline into a thin layer of sponge mounted on card and then dipping it into red paint to create a 'seal stamp', or by using a vegetable base—for example a half potato—on which you can cut out the cross shape, creating a potato print cross as your 'seal' stamp.

A Japanese cross

Bible link: Revelation 12:10–11

Then I heard a voice from heaven shout, 'Our God has shown his saving power, and his kingdom has come! God's own Chosen One has shown his authority. Satan accused our people in the presence of God day and night. Now he has been thrown out! Our people defeated Satan because of the blood of the Lamb and the message of God. They were willing to give up their lives.'

In his mysterious vision of the end of time, John writes about those who have faced great suffering as Christians but who in the end defeat the enemy by 'the blood of the Lamb', which is his way of describing Jesus' death on the cross.

Wondering about this Bible story

- I wonder how the first readers of this vision were affected by these words?
- I wonder how Christians can use Jesus death' on the cross to overcome the opposition they face?
- I wonder why some Christians choose to die rather than giving up on their faith?

The story of this cross

The first Christian missionary to Japan was Francis Xavier, a Roman Catholic, who went there in 1549. He wrote of the Japanese: 'These are the finest people yet discovered and it seems to me, among the believers, no people can be found to excel them.'

At first, Christianity was welcomed, but after about 50 years, there came a counter-reaction. The Emperor Hideyoshi issued a decree banning all missionaries and, in 1596, during a particularly fierce round of persecution, 26 Japanese and European Christians were crucified on bamboo crosses. There is a monument to their martyrdom in Nagasaki, where it happened. In fact, during this period of Japanese history, it is claimed that Japan had a higher number of martyrs in proportion to its Christian population than any other country in the world. Often the crucifixions that took place were of a particularly brutal nature and involved suspending victims upside-down over a pit.

Although today the Christian population of Japan is very tiny (about one per cent), it seems that the idea of the cross and its religious meaning is part of the Japanese consciousness, particularly in the area of art and literature. Christ crucified is seen primarily as a sufferer, and the cross is picked up as a symbol of tragic, innocent death, humanity on the rack, dashed hopes, self-sacrifice and the human tragedy of a child dying in the presence of his mother. It is perhaps no coincidence that the statue of Sadako—the young girl who died from radiation injuries after Hiroshima and whose origami crane folding is commemorated each year in the Peace Park—shows her with out-stretched arms in the shape of a cross.

Japanese understanding of Christian themes finds expression readily in literature and in theology. The fullest exposition of this theme is in the book entitled *Silence* by novelist Shusaku Endo. It deals with the sufferings of a character called Rodrigues, and many direct parallels are drawn with Christ. In the book, Endo also makes reference to the particular trial of faith to which many of the Japanese Christian martyrs were put.

To test whether people were Christian or not, they were asked to 'trample on' an image of Christ or Mary. Even if they had denied their Christian faith verbally, most could not bear to 'trample on' or 'rub out' these holy images when challenged in this way, and thus their true allegiance as believers was uncovered. The images used for this trial of faith were Japanese woodblock prints with the image of Mary and Jesus or Jesus on the cross on them. Some of these carvings, as well as bronze medallions of these sacred pictures known as *efumi*, are now housed at a museum in Oiso near Yokohama. On some, the faces have indeed been 'rubbed out'. It is said that some sympathetic Buddhist wood-carvers deliberately produced carvings without faces so that Christian friends could produce the apparently desecrated images and so save their lives.

This story of what happened to these images is brought out in the cross in this resource. The cross is a form of crucifix, but the shape of the body has been trampled or rubbed out. There is also a link to the suffering experienced by the people of Hiroshima and Nagasaki at the end of World War II. All that remained of some victims after the A-bomb explosion was their outline on the ground. Christians believe that the cross is God's participation in the immense sufferings of this world and that only a God who has experienced the worst can lead us through to the best as the result of his resurrection.

Crafting the cross

A craft idea for making a similar cross

Create a cross by folding and cutting a piece of A4 paper as in the instructions accompanying the Roman cross (pp. 84–85). When you have done this, draw an outline of a

body on the cross as in the picture on page 58. Cut out this shape so that the cross now has a body-shaped hole in it. Mount this on to a suitable background picture of people who are experiencing suffering or persecution in some way today, so that only their faces can be seen through the hole.

You may like to put a Bible verse next to this cross, such as 'He was hated and rejected; his life was filled with sorrow and terrible suffering' (Isaiah 53:3). Alternatively, alongside the cross, you could copy these Japanese characters that mean 'God is love'.

神 GOD

は IS

愛 LOVE

Here are some Japanese poems to go alongside the cross. They are haikus, which are a particular form of Japanese verse. Haikus are unrhymed and consist of three lines, containing five, seven and then five Japanese syllables respectively. The following six haikus are by Christian writers in Japan and have been translated into English. They are taken with permission from *A Procession of Prayers* by John Carden (Cassell WCC Publications, 1998).

Cold the winter night:
Somewhere in it,
one there was named Judas.

This spring breeze
A crown of thorns
And a reed.

The cross drags heavily
Tearing the earth
And its young grasses.

From Holy Scripture
One word, one phrase recalled,
And all his agony reappears.

A Holy Rood
I see the five wounds—
And a piercing cold besets me.

Ah, the fragrance of new grass!
I hear his footsteps coming—
Lord of the Resurrection!

Why not try to write your own haiku poems to go alongside the cross you have made?

An Australian cross

the cup from which I must drink. And you will be baptized just as I must! But it isn't for me to say who will sit at my right side and at my left. That is for God to decide.' When the ten other disciples heard this, they were angry with James and John. But Jesus called the disciples together and said: You know that those foreigners who call themselves kings like to order their people around. And their great leaders have full power over the people they rule. But don't act like them. If you want to be great, you must be the servant of all the others. And if you want to be first, you must be everyone's slave. The Son of Man did not come to be a slave master, but a slave who will give his life to rescue many people.

Jesus has to correct his disciples who think that in God's kingdom some people will be more important than others. In fact, his kingdom will be totally different. It will be a new sort of community based on serving one another and following the pattern set by Jesus, who went to the cross for all.

Bible link: Mark 10:35–45

James and John, the sons of Zebedee, came up to Jesus and asked, 'Teacher, will you do us a favour?' Jesus asked them what they wanted, and they answered, 'When you come into your glory, please let one of us sit at your right side and the other at your left.' Jesus told them, 'You don't really know what you're asking! Are you able to drink from the cup that I must soon drink from or be baptized as I must be baptized?' 'Yes, we are!' James and John answered. Then Jesus replied, 'You certainly will drink from

Wondering about this Bible story

- • I wonder why James and John wanted seats of honour in the kingdom?
- • I wonder whether they understood when Jesus spoke about a baptism and 'drinking from his cup'?
- • I wonder whether Christians can really be a new community in the way that Jesus describes?

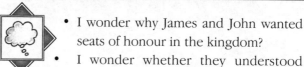

The story of this cross

The artwork of the Aboriginal culture of Australia is distinctive for its particular combinations of concentric circles, dots and curved lines. The circles, in particular, are sometimes used to represent the community and its innate strength.

Christians are not just a group of individuals who happen to believe the same things but are members of a new creation who, together, are called to express the character and life of Jesus to the world today. The Aboriginal culture is strongly communal and, as such, understands this truth better, perhaps, than many Christian groups in other parts of the world where life has become a highly individualized experience.

The full meaning of the symbols in Aboriginal art is never quite clear, and nor is it meant to be so. However, on the whole, the circles often represent sacred places or sites, the curved lines can express feelings such as pain or joy, and the dots represent individuals, each of whom God knows by name.

Crafting the cross

A craft idea for making a similar cross

On the BRF website, there is an example of this art form taken from a set of 'Stations of the Cross' by the Aboriginal artist Miriam-Rose Ungunm.

To make your own version of this cross from Australia, you will need to cut the basic cross outline out of card. Then you will need a series of cardboard or plastic tubes in various sizes, paints and some cotton buds.

- Dip the rims of the tubes into paint and use them to create a series of concentric circles on the cross. Reds, whites, blacks and yellows are the preferred colours.
- Use cotton buds dipped into the paint to add the dots and curved lines.
- The dots usually outline the circles and the ends of lines, and fill the spaces.

A Salvadorean cross

The story of this cross

This is a traditional cross from the country of El Salvador. It commemorates the life and witness of a young schoolteacher named Maria Christina Gomez. The pictures on the cross touch on a few significant events in her life. She was a very active member of her church and regularly met with others to work out how she and they could lead faithful Christian lives in El Salvador, a country in which there was much injustice, not least the deep divide between the rich and the poor.

One day, a van drew up outside the school where she worked, and she was taken away. Later that day she was found dead in another part of the city. No one knows why she was killed but Maria's friends did not want to forget her and the Christian example she had set. Her friends commissioned a 'picture cross' to celebrate her life and faith.

El Salvador is a small, crowded country in which unemployment is high and few can afford a proper education. As a nation, it also suffered from civil war for many years, until a peace treaty was eventually signed in 1992. In being commemorated, Maria is representative of the many unknown Christians who lived and died during that time.

The cross is decorated with various scenes from Maria's life: a depiction of her as a baby, using oxen to plough the land, going to school, picking coffee beans, and teaching. The cross reminds those who see it that the entirety of our life is of concern to God and that Jesus stands with us in the joys and pains of our everyday experiences and tasks.

Bible link: 1 John 3:16–18

We know what love is because Jesus gave his life for us. That's why we must give our lives for each other. If we have all we need and see one of our own people in need, we must have pity on that person, or else we cannot say we love God. Children, you show love for others by truly helping them, and not merely by talking about it.

John writes to remind Christians of how we are to love our neighbour and, as followers of Jesus, treat them very differently from the way many in the world treat others.

Wondering about this Bible story

- • I wonder why Christians are hated in some parts of the world?
- • I wonder what it means to give our lives for each other?
- • I wonder what it means truly to help others?

A craft idea for making a similar cross

Enlarge this black-and-white template of the cross and then colour it in.

- What can you tell about life in El Salvador from the different scenes painted on the cross?
- What do you think this cross meant and means to Maria's family and friends?

You could make a similar sort of cross to celebrate the life of someone you know, using scenes from his or her life. Choose other possible subjects for a traditional Salvadorian cross—for example, events that could illustrate the story of your church or school—and make a cross of your own design.

A Latin American cross

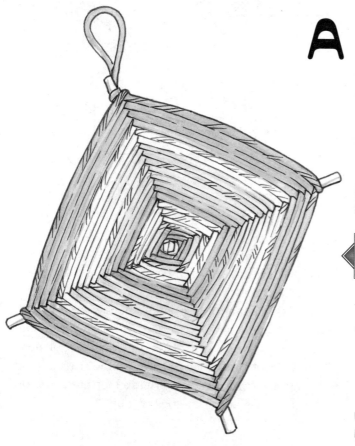

Wondering about this Bible story

- I wonder why processions and public festivals have always been so important to Christians?
- I wonder what impact such processions had on outsiders?
- I wonder what people today think when they see Christians marching with banners and crosses held high?

The story of this cross

Worship at special Christian festivals in central America is usually marked by plenty of extravagant colour and exuberant activity. During such festivals, local churches and various processional floats are decorated brightly and contain or carry symbols of the faith as part of the general celebrations.

One such decoration, typical of central America, is a diamond-shaped cross, known as the God's-eye cross. The eye is meant to symbolize the loving action of God who watches over Christians, protecting his people and guiding them into a Christ-like life. This cross can become a focus for prayer for the Christian family in Latin America, as we thank God for the gift of celebration they bring to the worldwide Church and for the growth of the Church in that part of the world in recent years.

Bible link: Psalm 68:4–8

Our God, you are the one who rides on the clouds, and we praise you. Your name is the Lord, and we celebrate as we worship you. Our God, from your sacred home you take care of orphans and protect widows. You find families for those who are lonely. You set prisoners free and let them prosper, but all who rebel will live in a scorching desert. You set your people free, and you led them through the desert. God of Israel, the earth trembled, and rain poured down. You alone are the God who rules from Mount Sinai.

Many psalms, like this one, were composed for singing during temple festivals and processions. The opening words of this psalm had first been used each time the people of God broke camp and set out on the next stage of their desert journey in Moses' day (see Numbers 10:35).

A craft idea for making a similar cross

Your group can make versions of this cross, using:
* ✠ Two kebab sticks (blunt the ends of the sticks for safety purposes)
* ✠ Sticky tape
* ✠ Brightly-coloured yarn

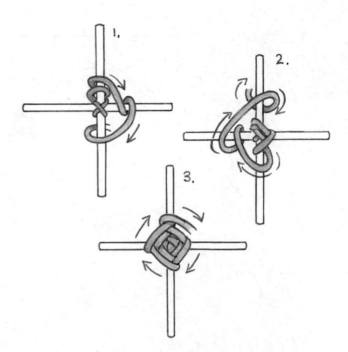

Tie the two kebab sticks together to make a cross with four equal 'arms' (see the diagram). A piece of garden twist is good for binding the two sticks together.

Attach one end of a piece of white yarn to the central point of the cross and then wrap the yarn under and around each arm of the cross in a diamond pattern. It is simpler to rotate the cross than the yarn as you do this.

After using it to make two or three complete circuits of the cross, cut the end of the yarn, attach a new colour and begin the circuits anew. Gradually, a pattern like an 'eye' will appear, especially if you keep

the different strands of thread tightly together.

Keep adding new strands of yarn in different colours, building up a bright, striped pattern. Each time you add another strand, you will make the diamond larger as you extend the circuits of new loops of wool out along the arms of the cross.

Attach a small piece of yarn in a loop at the top of the cross by which it can be hung up.

A Peruvian cross

so many sacrifices for the things they had done wrong?

- I wonder what those sacrifices tell us about what God thinks of wrongdoing?
- I wonder why Christians believe that Jesus' sacrifice is so much more powerful in its effect?

The story of this cross

 This Peruvian cross is from a tapestry that shows off the weaving skills of local people.

Most Peruvian tapestries are woven from 100 per cent sheep's wool, although alpaca (from a llama) is used in some regions. Weavers traditionally work as independent family units. It is the job of the women to do the carding and spinning, while the men weave. Tapestry styles are named according to the area in which they are initially produced.

Arpilleras were initially a Chilean tradition of making rags into small dolls which were then sewn or embroidered on to larger pieces of cloth. This technique was first introduced to Peru about 1980, when it was quickly adopted by the inhabitants of the shanty towns surrounding Lima.

There are three grades of tapestry:

- Street quality—made of virgin wool and natural dyes
- Special quality—made of pre-washed wool and aniline (chemical) dyes
- Signed—woven and signed by the master designers

Many of the traditional designs are geometric in nature, taken from stone temple carvings and codices, which are the picture books of the ancient Incas, Mayans and Aztecs.

Colours vary from soft and muted to bold and bright. Pale pastel colours normally indicate natural

Bible link: Hebrews 10:11–14

The priests do their work each day, and they keep on offering sacrifices that can never take away sins. But Christ offered himself as a sacrifice that is good for ever. Now he is sitting at God's right side, and he will stay there until his enemies are put under his power. By his one sacrifice he has for ever set free from sin the people he brings to God.

The writer of this letter contrasts the old ways of regular animal sacrifices with the once-for-all death of Jesus as the way to deal with the things we do wrong. All this is what the prophets of old foresaw.

Wondering about this Bible story

- I wonder why God in the Old Testament instructed his people to offer

dyes, while those with strong, bright hues indicate aniline dyes. Natural dyeing formulas are well-kept family secrets passed on from generation to generation. Some of the sources of these dyes are:

- Green/gold/yellow: tree bark and the fruit skin of the vejuco or vejigo (a fruit similar to a pomegranate)
- Red: from the dried bodies of the cochineal beetles found on the prickly pear cacti
- Black/grey/white: carefully selected and cleaned natural sheep's wool
- Blue: from the fresh green leaves of the indigo or anil bush
- Pink: from the bark of the South American pecan tree
- Brown: from black walnut hulls

Some of the Peruvian *arpilleras* have earned an international reputation as wall-hangings. There are unusual styles of weave that include dyed but unspun wool, individually arranged like brush strokes in a painting. The subject matter is often Peruvian scenes of everyday life, including local buildings, people in traditional costume, llamas and fiestas.

Behind the altar of the Anglican church in Arequipa in Peru is the woven cross tapestry pictured on page 67. It was produced by Quechua women who have become Christians. It is their response to what, for them, is the truth about Jesus. They use their own traditional browns on a white background. These are colours associated with their former animist beliefs, but they have also introduced a black, which for them symbolizes the greater power of the God who was in Christ and who died upon the cross. The South American Mission Society (SAMS) has close connections with this church and the work of Christians in Peru.

The Church in South America is growing and there is a passion for justice as well as a desire to share the good news with their neighbours.

Crafting the cross

A craft idea for making a similar cross

Using the picture as a guide, a group could work on a similar tapestry cross for their own church or school.

Following the style of an *arpillera*, pieces of rag could be rolled as small figures to be attached to the hanging around the cross.

Alternatively, cut out people and landscape shapes from felt cloth and glue them to the tapestry background. Use information from a local library or the Internet to choose colours and styles that will reflect local traditional costume. The group might even like to try to dye some white wool using some of the suggested natural sources listed above.

In order to express the message of this cross as understood by the Quechua, one of the following paraphrased versions of some appropriate Bible verses could be used:

On the cross Christ has disarmed evil of its power to hurt us (based on Colossians 2:15).

God made peace through his Son's death on the cross (based on Colossians 1:20).

Because of Christ's cross, the evil influence of this world on me is broken; I no longer have to give in to its empty charms (based on Galatians 6:14).

An Orthodox cross

- I wonder what the passers-by made of this signboard?
- I wonder why it was recorded in three languages?

The story of this cross

The Eastern and Oriental Orthodox churches constitute one of the three great Christian traditions, the other two being Roman Catholic and Protestant. The emphasis on 'right worship' (which is the meaning of 'Orthodox') has roots that extend back into the early centuries of the Church. It is characteristic of the Orthodox to give priority to liturgy, so they see mission as the invitation to all people to join with them in the unchanging worship of God, who is three in one. There is a great sense of majesty and mystery in the significance attached to symbols, pictures (known as icons), colours, sounds and smells that are integral elements in Orthodox services.

Orthodox believers have had to survive many pressures down the years, including those visited on them by hostile political systems such as that of Communist Russia, as well as the challenge of maintaining the faith in societies that are largely Muslim or Hindu. There are today some 200 million believers from the Orthodox tradition, found mainly around the Middle East, Egypt, Ethiopia, within the Commonwealth of Independent States (CIS) and in the former Communist countries of Eastern Europe.

The Orthodox churches have taken the lead in movement towards Christian unity. In fact, the Greek and Indian Orthodox Churches were among the founder members of the World Council of Churches.

The Orthodox cross is distinctive in that it usually includes an additional crosspiece on the lower half of the upright. This aligns with the segment of the cross

Bible link: John 19:16b–20

Jesus was taken away, and he carried his cross to a place known as 'The Skull'. In Aramaic this place is called 'Golgotha'. There Jesus was nailed to the cross, and on each side of him a man was also nailed to a cross. Pilate ordered the charge against Jesus to be written on a board and put above the cross. It read, 'Jesus of Nazareth, King of the Jews'. The words were written in Hebrew, Latin, and Greek.

John records how a title board was written in three languages to be nailed to the cross with Jesus.

Wondering about this Bible story

- I wonder why Pilate insisted on sticking with his chosen wording, despite opposition from the chief priests (see verses 21 and 22)?

to which Jesus' feet would have been nailed. There is also an extra crosspiece at the approximate point on the top half of the upright where, it is believed, the sign on which the title 'Jesus of Nazareth, King of the Jews' was written would have been nailed. Orthodox crosses are usually quite ornate and are very prominently displayed on and in all Orthodox churches. These crosses were on view, as though in silent defiance, atop the Kremlin buildings in Moscow even through Russia's 'atheistic' years in the 20th century.

Signing the cross

In many Christian traditions the priest or minister will make the sign of the cross as part of the liturgy or at the close of a service. In addition, it is often made at the beginning or end of a prayer, as a blessing or when the name of Jesus Christ is mentioned.

There are various ways in which the sign is made. In Western churches, the cross is signed either as a 'great sign' or a 'lesser sign'. The great sign involves the five outstretched fingers and thumb (symbols of the five wounds of Christ) of one hand, with which the worshipper touches his or her forehead, breast and left and right shoulders in turn. The thumb alone makes the lesser sign on forehead, lips and breast (to denote the desire for Christ in our thinking, speaking and feeling).

Since the seventh century, in the Eastern churches, the great sign has been made by using two fingers (the index and middle ones, which are symbolic of the fact that Christ was both God and human), which trace the cross from forehead to heart, and then from right to left shoulder. Another version of this sign involves the use of all five fingers curved, with the index and middle fingers touching the thumb—such a combination being a symbol of the Trinity. The shape of the cross is traced as before. Notice that in the Eastern tradition of signing, the 'horizontal beam' of the cross is always traced right to left, in contrast to the direction used in the Western tradition.

In the baptismal rite, new believers or young babies are marked with the sign of the cross on their forehead. The wording that usually accompanies this signing or blessing is 'In the name of the Father, and of the Son and of the Holy Spirit'.

Crafting the cross

A craft idea for making a similar cross

To make an Orthodox cross for yourself, you will need several layers of stiff card and some gold foil or wrapping paper.

- Using the cross template opposite, cut out at least four card outlines of the cross and glue or tape them together.
- Carefully wrap the foil or wrapping-paper around the cross, trying to ensure that the covering wraps the card cross as smoothly as possible.
- Next, roll up tiny balls of the foil and glue them on, particularly at the extremities of the cross, as additional decoration.
- The additional layers of card will help to give the cross a more three-dimensional aspect. The extra bulk of the additional layers will also make it easier for you to wrap the foil or paper around them.

A Celtic cross

This is the story of the apostle Paul preaching to the people of Athens at their great open-air debating ground on the Areopagus. He talked to them about creation and their own ideas of the gods, and even quoted local poetry.

Wondering about this Bible story

- I wonder why some people became so hostile when Paul talked about the resurrection? (See verse 32.)
- I wonder why Paul chose to talk about the cross in this indirect way on this occasion?
- I wonder whether Paul felt that his mission in Athens was successful or not?

The story of this cross

The year 1997 witnessed not only the 1,400th anniversary of the arrival of St Augustine in Britain on his mission from Rome to bring order and structure to the British Church but also the anniversary of the death of St Columba, the Celtic missionary. From his base on the island of Iona, Columba and his followers achieved remarkable success in taking the gospel to the peoples of the British Isles within a relatively short timespan. Many Christians today are finding inspiration in the lives and the prayers of these Celtic saints and see in their teaching and interpretation of the Christian faith a more truly 'British' expression of Christianity than the Roman version that eventually came to dominate the subsequent growth of the Church in the United Kingdom.

The Celtic understanding of the gospel and God's creation includes a strong sense of his presence in nature and in the everyday events of our human lives. There are prayers in the Celtic canon that acknowledge the divine provenance of all the

Bible link: Acts 17:22–28

People of Athens, I see that you are very religious. As I was going through your city and looking at the things you worship, I found an altar with the words, 'To an Unknown God'. You worship this God, but you don't really know him. So I want to tell you about him. This God made the world and everything in it. He is Lord of heaven and earth, and he doesn't live in temples built by human hands. He doesn't need help from anyone. He gives life, breath, and everything else to all people. From one person God made all nations who live on earth, and he decided when and where every nation would be. God has done all this, so that we will look for him and reach out and find him. He isn't far from any of us, and he gives us the power to live, to move, and to be who we are. 'We are his children,' just as some of your poets have said.

routines, banal and otherwise, of life. In expressions of Celtic intercession there is no dangerous division of sacred and secular, which can sometimes be a feature of the Christian faith in other traditions. The close intertwining of heavenly and earthly concerns is also expressed in the characteristic Celtic key patterns that are to be found at this period of early Church history. What seem at first glance to be broken lines in these designs prove in fact to be spirals, forming a continuous path that leads the observer through a complex maze to the sacred point where 'heaven' and 'earth' enfold each other.

These knotty designs are also depicted on the arms and uprights of Celtic crosses, linked by a circle that represents the earth.

Two of the most famous Celtic crosses are:

- The Bewcastle cross in Cumbria that dates from the late seventh century. It illustrates Christ trampling down wild beasts and also includes elaborate carvings of a tree, branches, fruits, birds and animals. This cross has runic inscriptions written on it.
- The Ruthwell cross in Dumfries, Scotland, which stands 18 feet high and has Gospel scenes carved into it. There are runic and Latin inscriptions on it.

Crafting the cross

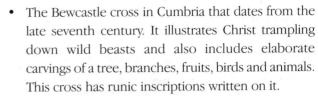

A craft idea for making a similar cross

In order to create your own Celtic cross, you will need:
- A template of the cross, photocopied on to card
- Glue
- Coloured string
- Crayons or pastels in natural greens, blues and browns
- Split peas or lentils

- Apply glue to the surface of the cross.
- Slowly lay coloured string on the surface, weaving it in intersecting patterns as shown in the template opposite.
- Link up the end of your string to the point at which you started, to complete 'the eternity of the maze'.
- Colour in the rest of the surface of the cross with the greens, blues and browns of nature to emphasize the strong connection between the truth of Calvary and the experience of our day-to-day lives on earth.
- Stick split peas or lentils where the circles meet to give the cross an extra tactile dimension.

The Taizé cross

Bible link: Isaiah 2:1–5

This is the message that I was given about Judah and Jerusalem: In the future, the mountain with the Lord's temple will be the highest of all. It will reach above the hills; every nation will rush to it. Many people will come and say, 'Let's go to the mountain of the Lord God of Jacob and worship in his temple.' The Lord will teach us his Law from Jerusalem, and we will obey him. He will settle arguments between nations. They will beat their swords and their spears into rakes and shovels; they will never make war or attack one another. People of Israel, let's live by the light of the Lord.

The Old Testament book of Isaiah gives us this vision of how, one day, all nations will come together and learn to walk in the light of God's peaceful ways.

Wondering about this Bible story

- I wonder how the prophet thought this vision would be fulfilled?
- I wonder how this connects with the story of Jesus and his cross?
- I wonder if there is any sign that this vision is coming true?

The story of this cross

One of the ways in which Christians have tried to express their faith down the ages is by living in communities and reaching out from such centres of prayer and worship to meet the needs of people in the world around them. Today, the gifts and ministries of such communities often cross traditional denominational boundaries, and they have become a focus of unity and shared Christian faith for many, particularly young people, who increasingly feel isolated from the established churches.

One such community, founded by Brother Roger in France, is Taizé. The influence of its music and spirituality has now reached many parts of the world and touched believers of widely differing traditions. Groups come to Taizé from all over Europe and beyond. They stay for short periods and share in the day-to-day work and prayer life of the monks, meeting others from a variety of backgrounds and cultures who are seeking to discover afresh or deepen their spiritual lives. Through the experience of talking and worshipping together, those who go to Taizé grow in their understanding of God and of each other. In many ways, Taizé and places like it serve as symbols of hope for the future of the Christian family because they act as catalysts for the recommitment of many to the work of the gospel.

What has become known as the Taizé cross is a visual sign of this unity and the commitment of people to work out the meaning of the Easter event for the world today. Many groups that travel to Taizé from the United Kingdom have been very moved by what they experience there. They retain strong memories of candle-lit services in Taizé's great 'Cathedral of Reconciliation'.

Crafting the cross

A craft idea for making a similar cross

The basic shape of the cross is covered with a collage of different pictures representing all the people groups for whom Christ died.

To make this cross individually or as a group activity, you will need a large, firm version of the cross, possibly constructed or cut from cardboard or something stronger.

On to this cross, stick as wide-ranging a selection of pictures, drawings and other artwork as possible.

Try to include pictures of the members of the group and use a mission magazine, such as *Yes* from CMS, to find photographs of people from different parts of God's world, particularly those with whom your group or school has special links and those who are in particular need at the time of your taking part in this activity.

It is often effective to stick a picture of Jesus at the centre, perhaps from an illustration of an icon or from one of the great paintings of the life of Christ. Christmas or Easter cards may supply examples.

The cross should, like the Taizé community itself, symbolize the unity of the worldwide Christian family and hope for a divided and broken world.

An Irish cross

The story of this cross

Bridget, the daughter of a nobleman and a Christian slave, was born in the middle of the fifth century in Ireland. She was, by all accounts, a spirited young woman and one who, from an early age, cared little for personal property. Throughout her life she was well known as being someone who gave away as much as she could to those in need.

Bridget began a Christian abbey at Kildare. Her fellow nuns were drawn from every social rank, ranging from princesses to slaves. The community included men, over whom Bridget, as abbess, held authority. This Celtic model contrasts with the Roman pattern followed in England within which the male bishops held supreme sway. Bridget's generous hospitality to people who were poor or unwell was renowned, and there are many miracles attributed to her saintliness. She became, like Patrick before her, a patron of poets, craftsmen and healers, and the church at Kildare acquired, in the years after her death, a reputation for its splendour and beauty. As a saint she is associated chiefly with arts and learning as well as the work of a dairymaid, which had been her job when she was a slave-girl.

According to legend, Bridget used to weave crosses, which were then tied with ribbons. These she gave as gifts, along with words of love and encouragement, to whomever she met on her journeys.

Today, small replicas of this cross can be found in many Irish homes because it is believed that they act as protection against danger and evil. Bridget's feast day is 1 February. Here is part of the poem known as 'Bridget's feast':

I should welcome the poor to my feast,
For they are God's children.
I should welcome the sick to my feast,

Bible link: Luke 6:37–38

Jesus said: Don't judge others, and God won't judge you. Don't be hard on others, and God won't be hard on you. Forgive others, and God will forgive you. If you give to others, you will be given a full amount in return. It will be packed down, shaken together, and spilling over into your lap. The way you treat others is the way you will be treated.

Jesus calls his disciples to a life of giving and forgiving. Only as they let go can their hands be free enough to receive all that God wants to give them.

Wondering about this Bible story

- I wonder why people find it so hard to let go and to give to those in need?
- I wonder what sort of blessing God does give to those who give to others?
- I wonder what Jesus would say to those people who feel they ought to keep something back, just in case?

For they are God's joy.
Let the poor sit with Jesus at the highest place
And the sick dance with the angels.
God bless the poor;
God bless the sick,
And bless our human race.
God bless our food,
God bless our drink,
All homes, O God, embrace.

Crafting the cross

A craft idea for making a similar cross

To make a woven cross like St Bridget's from coloured paper, you will need four long narrow loops of paper, which can then be woven together by carefully slipping the ends of each strip through and around the loops of the other strips (see the diagram opposite).

To complete the cross, tie off the loose ends with coloured ribbon just as Bridget would have done.

- Cut an A4 piece of paper into four strips, each 2cm in width, and trim the ends to make points.
- Fold each strip in half.
- Join the four strips together as shown, overlapping so that they hold together.
- Glue the loose ends together and decorate.

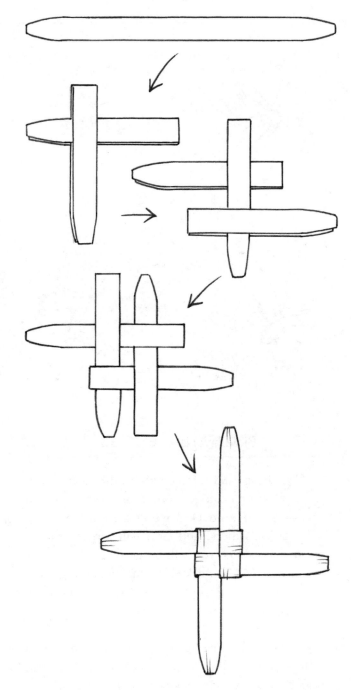

A Greek cross

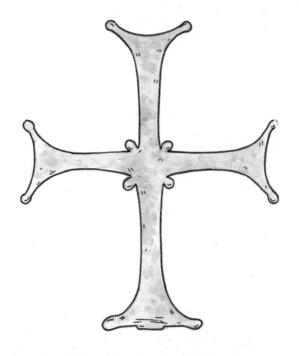

- I wonder why the cross attracts people of all types and from all places?

The story of this cross

The cross that has four equal segments or 'arms' is known as the Greek cross, and is used as a basic element in many other cross designs. It is sometimes surrounded by a circle and embodies then the symbolism of Jesus' death reaching out and touching the world at all four points of the compass. Sometimes, a simple Greek cross is decorated with trefoils at the end of each arm. It is then known as a cross *boutonnée*. The trefoil symbolically represents the Holy Trinity.

The cross with four equal arms is, of course, the one adopted by the Red Cross, symbolizing the bringing of hope, healing and humanitarian aid to those who are victims of wars or natural disasters. (For more on this cross, see 'A Swiss cross', pp. 88–89.)

The shape of the Greek cross is a common pattern for the ground-plan of churches in the Orthodox tradition. An Orthodox church usually consists of a square, a central tower and four 'arms' or spaces of equal length that extend geographically north, south, east and west from it.

Bible link: John 12:27–33

Jesus said: Now I am deeply troubled, and I don't know what to say. But I must not ask my Father to keep me from this time of suffering. In fact, I came into the world to suffer. So Father, bring glory to yourself. A voice from heaven then said, 'I have already brought glory to myself, and I will do it again!' When the crowd heard the voice, some of them thought it was thunder. Others thought an angel had spoken to Jesus. Then Jesus told the crowd, 'That voice spoke to help you, not me. This world's people are now being judged, and the ruler of this world is already being thrown out! If I am lifted up above the earth, I will make everyone want to come to me.' Jesus was talking about the way he would be put to death.

Shortly before his death, Jesus heard God's voice of reassurance. His death would be the way in which all the people of the world would be drawn to God.

Wondering about this Bible story

- I wonder why God needed to speak these words to Jesus?
- I wonder how the cross can be the way that 'the ruler of this world' is 'thrown out'?

Crafting the cross

A craft idea for making a similar cross

The four shapes on page 78 are jigsaw pieces. When fitted together, they will make a Greek cross. Copy these pieces on to stiff card and then try to put them together so that they form a perfect, symmetrical cross.

It is not as easy as it might seem, and some of the pieces will need to be turned over so that you can achieve it. Enlarged versions of the jigsaw pieces could become bases on to which you could fix pictures or photos to create a mosaic version of the Greek cross.

The pictures or photos could illustrate situations from anywhere in the world. In fact, the jigsaw pieces on this sheet could be taken as representing some of the continents outside Europe. They have been arranged in the artwork to produce precisely this geographical pattern or effect. (The continents are North and South America, Asia and Africa.)

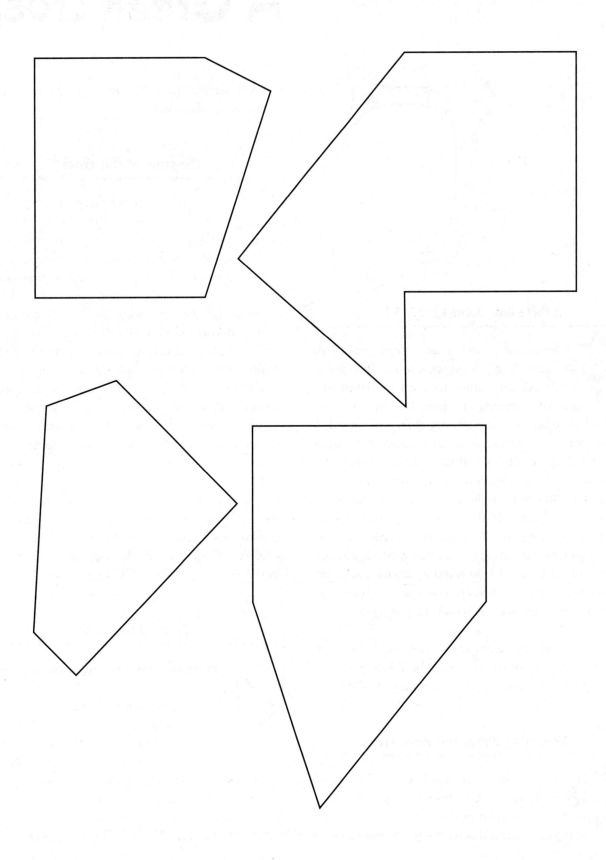

Reproduced with permission from *A–Cross the World* published by BRF 2004 (1 84101 264 5)

A Finnish cross

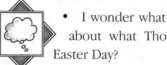

Wondering about this Bible story

- I wonder what the other disciples felt about what Thomas said on that first Easter Day?
- I wonder why Jesus made a special appearance for Thomas?
- I wonder if Thomas the doubter ended up with perhaps a stronger faith than even some of the others?

The story of this cross

The St Thomas Mass is now well-known in Scandinavia and northern Europe. It is a new, urban approach to sharing the good news of Jesus. The first such service was held in Helsinki, Finland, in 1988. It takes the form of traditional Lutheran worship that has been influenced by new styles of music, prayer and liturgy, particularly those of the Taizé community in France and the Orthodox tradition of Eastern Europe. It is designed especially with the outsider in mind—the sort of worshipper who may have drifted away from the traditional church and who is looking for new, contemporary ways to express his or her search for meaning in life. It is for this reason that the service is named after Thomas the apostle. He symbolizes today's would-be disciple who often has more questions than answers in his or her understanding of the Christian faith.

A large team of lay leaders and some clergy known collectively as the Thomas Community runs the service. It is an ecumenical venture and combines elements from many church traditions. It aims to be accessible and relevant, in contrast to the more archaic or formal liturgies of the established churches that are failing to attract today's younger generation. The service includes space for silence, symbols, storytelling

Bible link: John 20:24–28

Although Thomas the Twin was one of the twelve disciples, he wasn't with the others when Jesus appeared to them. So they told him, 'We have seen the Lord!' But Thomas said, 'First, I must see the nail scars in his hands and touch them with my finger. I must put my hand where the spear went into his side. I won't believe unless I do this!' A week later the disciples were together again. This time, Thomas was with them. Jesus came in while the doors were still locked and stood in the middle of the group. He greeted his disciples and said to Thomas, 'Put your finger here and look at my hands! Put your hand into my side. Stop doubting and have faith!' Thomas replied, 'You are my Lord and my God!'

Thomas wouldn't believe that Jesus had risen from the dead until he saw Jesus for himself. This happened eight days after Easter Sunday and became a moment of deep, life-changing worship for Thomas.

and a variety of musical styles. There is less stress on appealing to the intellect and a new emphasis on the mystery of the faith. People are encouraged to move about within the service and share experiences and doubts. Above all, a deliberate effort is made to help newcomers to feel welcome in a church environment, which, for many, can be an alien and uncomfortable place nowadays. The organizers usually provide time for participants to enjoy a meal together at some point in the experience.

A simple altar is the focus for the worship. On this altar will be a St Thomas cross, carved from local wood and encompassing an intricate pattern of delicate spirals, which are shavings that curl off from the arms and upright of the cross. It mirrors, perhaps, the holy chaos of the mass itself and the beautiful interweaving of the many elements in the worship, as each participant comes, with his or her own portmanteau of doubts and questions, towards the cross of Christ until he or she arrives at that moment when, like Thomas, he or she can bow before Jesus and say, 'My Lord and my God'. Such altars and crosses have been set up in secular venues too, such as shopping centres and sports stadia. The St Thomas Mass is proving very popular and is now commonly offered in all parts of Finland.

Crafting the cross

A craft idea for making a similar cross

To make your own version of this important cross, you will need some pieces of light wood (such as balsa wood) and some shiny, coloured paper.

- Fix two pieces of the wood together as a cross (see the picture on page 79) by cutting a tiny section out of one length at the point where the two pieces are meant to cross. Glue the two pieces together.
- Cut the shiny paper into thin strips, the same width as the upright and crosspiece. Using a pencil, gently stroke various lengths of the paper until they curl in varying degrees. Stick these along the crosspiece and up the upright, following a similar pattern to that in the picture.
- Alternatively, if you prefer to make this cross simply in two dimensions for display purposes, paper quilling would produce a similar result.

A Maltese cross

Paul was being taken as a prisoner to Rome, to appear before the emperor. His ship ran aground on the island of Malta but he was able to demonstrate that God was still with him, and brought God's healing to the local governor's family.

Wondering about this Bible story

- I wonder what the other passengers felt about the prisoner Paul?
- I wonder whether the miracle of the snakebite led to some people believing in Jesus?
- I wonder what Publius the governor thought about Paul and his story about Jesus?

The story of this cross

Malta lies in the Mediterranean Sea between Sicily and north Africa. The island was virtually cut off for part of World War II; the nearest Allied bases were nearly a thousand miles away, whereas Italian bombers could reach it from an airfield only 60 miles away. Most people thought that Malta would fall. It endured massive bombing and a siege for over two years. The people suffered but they were determined not to give in. King George VI of Great Britain awarded the George Cross to the entire population on 16 April 1942. The cross—their very own Maltese Cross—has special significance for the islanders.

If Malta had fallen, Nazi forces would have had complete control of the Mediterranean and north Africa, and would have been able to cut off British sea routes. Allied ships, in what came to be known as 'the Malta convoys', struggled through to reach the island. Many ships and lives were lost. On 15 August 1942, Allied ships finally broke the blockade and Malta was saved. The governor of the island at the

Bible link: Acts 27:43—28:5, 7–9

Captain Julius wanted to save Paul's life, and he did not let the soldiers do what they planned. Instead, he ordered everyone who could swim to dive into the water and head for shore. Then he told the others to hold on to planks of wood or parts of the ship. At last, everyone safely reached shore. When we came ashore, we learnt that the island was called Malta. The local people were very friendly, and they welcomed us by building a fire, because it was rainy and cold. After Paul had gathered some wood and had put it on the fire, the heat caused a snake to crawl out, and it bit him on the hand. When the local people saw the snake hanging from Paul's hand, they said to each other, 'This man must be a murderer! He didn't drown in the sea, but the goddess of justice will kill him anyway.' Paul shook the snake off into the fire and wasn't harmed...

The governor of the island was named Publius, and he owned some of the land around there. Publius was very friendly and welcomed us into his home for three days. His father was in bed, sick with fever and stomach trouble, and Paul went to visit him. Paul healed the man by praying and placing his hands on him. After this happened, everyone on the island brought their sick people to Paul, and they were all healed.

time said, 'The heroism and devotion of a brave people will long be famous in history.'

The cross is made up of what could be described as four 'arrow heads', the points of which meet together at the cross's centre. Traditionally, the four arms of the cross have stood for justice, perseverance, temperance and fortitude. Christians believe that these qualities should also mark the lives of those who follow Jesus, and that those who know the forgiveness that the cross of Christ can bring can also receive God's Holy Spirit, who will produce these and other gifts in the lives of believers.

Since the apostle Paul was shipwrecked on Malta, the islanders trace the beginning of their history to that visit and the subsequent conversion of its governor or prefect.

This cross was originally the symbol of the Knights of St John of Jerusalem. The points stand for the knightly virtues of piety, loyalty, generosity, courage, modesty, contempt of death, helpfulness to the poor and respect for the church. This cross is perhaps most commonly associated today with St John Ambulance, who use it as their logo. Theirs is a work of mercy—helping people who are in distress. The eight points of the cross are, in this context, sometimes linked to the Beatitudes—the eight sayings of Jesus that all begin with the phrase 'God blesses those people who…' (see Matthew 5:2–12).

Crafting the cross

A craft idea for making a similar cross

Using the template below, cut out the cross in stiff card, and cover it in silver foil or shiny, coloured paper. At each of the eight points of the cross, why not write down or illustrate one of the fruit of the Holy Spirit—other than love— as outlined in Galatians 5:22–23? Inscribe 'love', which is actually listed first in that verse, at the centre of the cross.

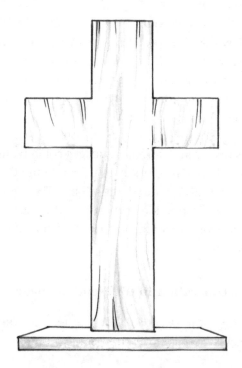

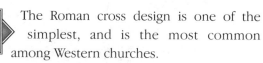

A Roman cross

The story of this cross

The Roman cross design is one of the simplest, and is the most common among Western churches.

An interesting discovery based on this cross was found in the catacombs (underground burial chambers) in Rome, where the Christians of the first century met in secret to worship and to avoid being caught by the Roman authorities who were hostile to the Christian faith. It was in the form of the following mysterious acrostic in Latin. An acrostic is a word square that reads the same set of words both horizontally and vertically.

$$R \quad O \quad T \quad A \quad S$$
$$O \quad P \quad E \quad R \quad A$$
$$T \quad E \quad N \quad E \quad T$$
$$A \quad R \quad E \quad P \quad O$$
$$S \quad A \quad T \quad O \quad R$$

The Latin means nothing special in itself: it translates as 'Arepo the sower holds the wheels with effort'. However, if all the letters are rearranged, then it creates a cross formed by the two words Pater Noster, centred on the 'N' and with two 'A's and two 'O's distributed one at each end. The acrostic turns out to be an early Christian coded version of the Lord's Prayer! (See overleaf for a diagram.)

'Pater Noster' are the first two words of the prayer in Latin, meaning 'Our Father'. The 'O' and the 'A' stand for the words 'Alpha' and 'Omega', which are the first and last letters of the Greek alphabet in Latin script. This is what Jesus calls himself in the book of Revelation (1:8). He is the beginning and the end, the first and the last—the A to Z of life!

Bible link: Psalm 85:8–13

I will listen to you, Lord God, because you promise peace to those who are faithful and no longer foolish. You are ready to rescue everyone who worships you, so that you will live with us in all your glory. Love and loyalty will come together; goodness and peace will unite. Loyalty will sprout from the ground; justice will look down from the sky above. Our Lord, you will bless us; our land will produce wonderful crops. Justice will march in front, making a path for you to follow.

The psalmist describes how God speaks peace to his people. It is a peace that involves love, loyalty and goodness coming together. God's rescue plan—our salvation—lies at the place where these three qualities meet.

Wondering about this Bible story

- I wonder how the psalmist believes that peace will come one day?
- I wonder what Jesus' cross might have to do with love, loyalty and goodness?
- I wonder if there can ever be real peace without goodness, or love without loyalty?

```
                    A
                    P
                    A
                    T
                    E
                    R
A  P  A  T  E  R  N  O  S  T  E  R  O
                    O
                    S
                    T
                    E
                    R
                    O
```

But that is not all. There are other hidden messages in this simple piece of early Christian graffiti. It contains a type of code to encourage the believers who were facing persecution at the hands of Nero and other Roman emperors.

At the centre of the acrostic is a cross made by the word 'tenet', which, in Latin, means 'he keeps' or 'he holds'.

```
            T
            E
    T  E  N  E  T
            E
            T
```

Furthermore, the 'T' would be recognized as the usual shape of the cross on which the Romans used to execute criminals. It is known as the tau cross. In the acrostic, each of these 'T's is surrounded by an Alpha and Omega. What an encouragement it must have been for frightened Christians to discover this secret message!

Perhaps a group of children and adults could follow this coded example and write their own Lord's Prayer in disguise? Can the group make a similar acrostic using English words, working only with the eight different letters involved in 'Our Father: O - U - R - F - A - T - H - E'? In some parts of the world today it isn't safe to be too public about Christian commitment, just as it wasn't for the first Christians in Rome.

The Lord's Prayer as recorded in Luke 11 and Matthew 6 is the special prayer that Jesus taught to his followers. It is also a pattern for prayer and one that is used all around God's world in its various forms and languages, linking up the family of believers from every nation.

The following versions of the opening two words of this prayer in different languages could be used to create other word crosses, to celebrate the Christian family at prayer around the globe. This can serve both as an inspiration to prayer and an encouragement to world mission, so that this family may keep on growing.

Our Father in different languages

Here are the words 'Our Father' in different languages. Perhaps you know some more?

Pater Noster	(Latin)
Padre Nuestro	(Spanish)
Notre Père	(French)
Mi Atyank	(Hungarian)
Jsä Meidan	(Finnish)
Vor Fader	(Danish)
Fader Wår	(Swedish)
Bisum Babamüs	(Turkish)
Abi-nu	(Hebrew in Latin script)
Ein Tad	(Welsh)
Unser Vater	(German)
Otesh Nash	(Russian in Latin script)
Cita bo	(Hottentot—South Africa)
Babu Yetu	(Swahili)
A Athair	(Irish)
Ojeze Nasz	(Polish)
Abuna	(Arabic in Latin script)
Pater Nostro	(Italian)

Crafting the cross

A craft idea for making a similar cross

This basic cross design can be made from one piece of A4 paper. You will need scissors and a pen or pencil.

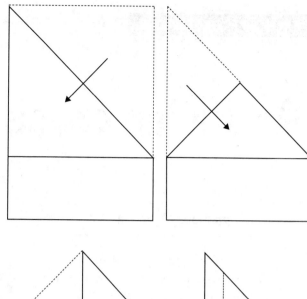

This cross can be made and used in a number of contexts—as part of an all-age service during which, at some point, the whole congregation is involved in making the cross; as an illustration 'up front' used as part of a talk; or as an activity for a small group, leading to sharing and prayer.

On a piece of A4 paper, draw a circle of about 5cm in diameter. Position it as shown in the diagram below, 7.5cm down from the top edge of the paper and centrally between the two sides.

◄ 7.5cm

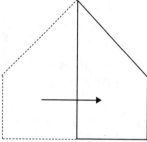
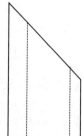

Inside this circle, each person could either write his or her name, draw himself or herself, or write about/draw people or situations that each wishes to bring to the cross in prayer.

To create the cross, follow these instructions and the diagram opposite.

- Fold the top right-hand corner to meet the left-hand edge.
- Fold the top left to meet the right-hand edge (creating a house shape).
- Fold the 'house' in half.
- Cut away the paper 2cm in from the right and about 3cm from the long edge.
- Unfold the paper to reveal the cross, with the circle at the point where the upright and crosspiece meet.

An Italian cross

Bible link: Psalm 8:1–6

Our Lord and Ruler, your name is wonderful everywhere on earth! You let your glory be seen in the heavens above. With praises from children and from tiny infants, you have built a fortress. It makes your enemies silent, and all who turn against you are left speechless. I often think of the heavens your hands have made, and of the moon and stars you put in place. Then I ask, 'Why do you care about us humans? Why are you concerned for us weaklings?' You made us a little lower than you yourself, and you have crowned us with glory and honour. You let us rule everything your hands have made. And you put all of it under our power.

The psalmist marvels at the beauty of creation and is amazed that God has given human beings such an important place in it all.

Wondering about this Bible story

- I wonder why looking at the stars makes many people wonder about God?
- I wonder how it is that praise from children and tiny infants can silence the voice of God's enemies? (see Psalm 8:2)
- I wonder how we should care for God's world?

The story of this cross

The famous icon cross of San Damiano hangs today in the Chapel of St Clare in Assisi. Painted originally in the 12th century in Umbria, Italy, it used to hang in the Church

of San Damiano, which is where it gained its name.

Once, the son of a wealthy merchant came into this ruined church to pray. His name was Giovanni Francesco Bernadone and, as he knelt before this particular icon of Christ, he heard a voice telling him to 'rebuild my Church'. This was the beginning of the story of St Francis and how he abandoned his inheritance to found a simple monastic order, which was devoted to proclaiming the gospel and rebuilding the Church, which is the people of God.

The cross is full of remarkable detail. There are at least 31 figures painted in the scenes around the central figure. This gives a sense that Christ is not only in the outstretched position of a sufferer, but he is also there holding all the stories of these people together in a welcoming embrace. The cross is elaborately framed by decorative moulding, which symbolizes the separation of the things of earth and the things of heaven. The onlooker is being invited to glimpse what the cross really means beyond the stark horrors of the human crucifixion.

Above the figure of Christ, angels welcome the triumphant risen Jesus out of the darkness of the tomb into heaven, while the right hand of God the Father reaches down in blessing on the whole event. More angels frame the crosspiece of the icon, reminding us of those things that 'angels would like to know more about' (1 Peter 1:12) and of the legions of angels that the Bible says Christ could have called to his aid, had he chosen (Matthew 26:53).

Left and right of the cross are people in medieval costume. These are the people of the artist's own day—contemporaries for whom the cross was still a talking point, a place of repentance and the inspiration for a new beginning. The smaller figures could well symbolize the humble and childlike response that such a new beginning involves. Finally, below the figure of Christ are the saints and apostles of every age who, under his authority, go out from the foot of the cross to tell this greatest of stories, which Christians believe to be the world's true story.

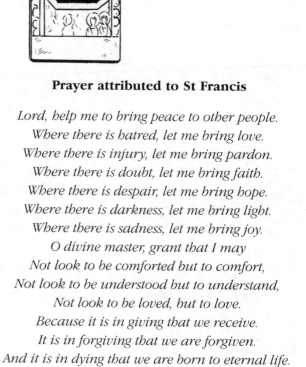

Crafting the cross

 A craft idea for making a similar cross

Enlarge the template provided on this page and mount it on a firm card base.

Now colour your own San Damiano cross prayerfully and carefully as a gift for someone, for another group of people or as part of a special display.

Given the cross's connection with the story of St Francis, it might also be appropriate to add the words of St Francis' most famous prayer, either on the back of the cross or on an accompanying card.

Prayer attributed to St Francis

Lord, help me to bring peace to other people.
Where there is hatred, let me bring love.
Where there is injury, let me bring pardon.
Where there is doubt, let me bring faith.
Where there is despair, let me bring hope.
Where there is darkness, let me bring light.
Where there is sadness, let me bring joy.
O divine master, grant that I may
Not look to be comforted but to comfort,
Not look to be understood but to understand,
Not look to be loved, but to love.
Because it is in giving that we receive.
It is in forgiving that we are forgiven.
And it is in dying that we are born to eternal life.
Amen

Reproduced with permission from A–Cross the World published by BRF 2004 (1 84101 264 5)

A Swiss cross

Bible link: Luke 10:30–35

Jesus replied: As a man was going down from Jerusalem to Jericho, robbers attacked him and grabbed everything he had. They beat him up and ran off, leaving him half dead. A priest happened to be going down the same road. But when he saw the man, he walked by on the other side. Later a temple helper came to the same place. But when he saw the man who had been beaten up, he also went by on the other side. A man from Samaria then came travelling along that road. When he saw the man, he felt sorry for him and went over to him. He treated his wounds with olive oil and wine and bandaged them. Then he put him on his own donkey and took him to an inn, where he took care of him. The next morning he gave the innkeeper two silver coins and said, 'Please take care of the man. If you spend more than this on him, I will pay you when I return.'

In reply to a lawyer's question, 'Who are my neighbours?' Jesus told the parable of the good Samaritan.

Wondering about this Bible story

- • I wonder who the lawyer felt was his neighbour before he heard Jesus' story?
- • I wonder why the priest and temple helper passed by on the other side?
- • I wonder how we can do the same as the man from Samaria?

The story of this cross

It was midsummer in 1859. Jean Henri Dunant, the son of a Swiss businessman, was travelling across Italy on a special mission that involved contacting the emperor Napoleon the Third. The emperor was difficult to track down, however, since at the time he was busy fighting a war against the Austrians. By the time Jean Dunant arrived in the little town of Solferino, one of the fiercest battles of that particular campaign had just been completed, and he was greeted by the appalling sight of thousands of wounded soldiers lying untended across the battlefield. Jean determined that something must be done to relieve such widespread suffering.

Forgetting his original mission, Jean plunged into the work of rescue, persuading others to join him. This whole experience inspired him with the idea of setting up a volunteer service to help the wounded in time of war. In order to publicize his plan, he wrote a book called *A memory of Solferino*, and his story stirred people to action.

In 1863, a committee of five Swiss citizens, including Jean Dunant, formed a society 'to aid the wounded' and laid the foundations of the greatest humanitarian movement the world has known.

A year later, an international convention was held in Geneva where rules were drawn up concerning those who were injured in wars. The title 'The Red Cross' was chosen, and the sign of a red cross on a white background became the recognized symbol of the organization. This is, in fact, the reverse of the Swiss national flag—a compliment to Jean Dunant's pioneering involvement.

Jean extended his work by helping to draw up the Geneva Convention, which deals with prisoners of war. Although full implementation of this only came after his death, Jean was among the first recipients of the Nobel Peace Prize (in 1901) to mark his work.

In Muslim countries, the Red Cross took the sign of the Red Crescent, and, in Iran, that of the Red Lion and Sun. In each case, however, these signs stand for the same humanitarian concerns—the relief of suffering wherever it may be found. Wherever these symbols are displayed, the wounded and all who minister to them are protected by international agreement. The Red Cross breaks through all barriers of class, race and colour.

The Red Cross is not entirely concerned with wars. Its peacetime charter includes first aid, nursing and welfare work, and relief in disasters. In recent times it has also concerned itself with international campaigns, in particular the banning of the use of land mines. The blood transfusion service, started in 1921, owes its origins to the British Red Cross Society.

The use of a cross for humanitarian work has, of course, great significance for those who have been brought up within a Christian tradition. The compassion and healing ministry of Christ relate directly to the nature of the society's work. For Muslims, however, the use of a cross, with its clear Christian links, can be a problem. Although the use of the Red Crescent has met this objection to an extent, nevertheless there are moves to adopt an additional emblem, which would safeguard all sensibilities. For more information, visit the website for the International Red Cross: www.icrc.org

Crafting the cross

A craft idea for making a similar cross

As a group, collect pictorial examples of Red Cross work around the world, including information about current war zones and disarmament issues. These could be arranged as a collage in the white areas around the red cross.

NB: Sensitivity needs to be observed for those who are not working within a Christian context.

A cross of nails

Bible link: 2 Corinthians 5:14–15, 17–19

We are ruled by Christ's love for us. We are certain that if one person died for everyone else, then all of us have died. And Christ did die for all of us. He died so we would no longer live for ourselves, but for the one who died and was raised to life for us...

Anyone who belongs to Christ is a new person. The past is forgotten, and everything is new. God has done it all! He sent Christ to make peace between himself and us, and he has given us the work of making peace between himself and others. What we mean is that God was in Christ, offering peace and forgiveness to the people of this world. And he has given us the work of sharing his message about peace.

Paul writes here about the meaning of the cross. It is the place where the old selfish ways can die and where people can make a new start in life with Jesus. He focuses on the new friendship and togetherness with God that the cross makes possible. This 'making peace' is what Christians should pass on to others.

Wondering about this Bible story

- I wonder how the cross can become a new start for Christians?
- I wonder what it means to be together with and friends of God?
- I wonder how Christians can pass this experience on to other people?

The story of this cross

A cross of nails lies at the very heart of the ministry of Coventry Cathedral. This cross has been a prime symbol of reconciliation since it was first created after the destruction of the old cathedral during the bombing of Coventry in World War II. It has been used in various ways to signify the call to peace, healing and friendship over many years. There are currently over fifty 'Cross of Nails' centres located around the world, working in their own unique ways to bring reconciliation to the various communities and nations in which they are found.

The Reverend Arthur Wales, a vicar from Coventry, made the first crosses of this kind. He picked up nails from the cathedral ruins on the day after the bombing in 1940; he soldered them and had them silvered to make a shining cross. It became a cross of hope which, alongside a cross made from two charred beams from the roof of the destroyed building, visually spelt out the meaning of reconciliation. Today this cross is worn by the clergy and vergers of Coventry Cathedral and is a symbol of inspiration, friendship and co-operation. Individuals and groups have been given such crosses to acknowledge, consolidate or give added motivation to their work in bringing together people or communities divided by hatred and suspicion.

The cross of nails consists of three nails. It is

widely believed that three nails were used to fix Christ to the cross. They represent the daily 'crucifixions' that take place in our personal and public lives. However, Good Friday led to Easter Day, and the shining cross inspires us to walk in hope the road that leads from pain to joy. The vertical nail symbolizes reconciliation (the bringing together) between the individual and God, as well as the reconciliation of the individual to himself or herself. The horizontal nails represent all our interpersonal relationships, which, through God (represented by the vertical nail), can bring healing and a new start.

Christians remember that Jesus grew up as a carpenter's son and would have been no stranger to nails and wood. The cross reminds us that he can take the various characteristics, good and bad, of each one of us and turn them into something beautiful, just as a master carpenter can create a beautiful piece of furniture from what sometimes looks like fairly unpromising material.

What areas of conflict, mistrust and division are there in your neighbourhood, church or school? Discuss and explore with members of your group how they can be peacemakers and reconcilers in those difficult situations.

For more information on the cross of nails, contact:

The Director of the International Centre for Reconciliation
7 Priory Row
Coventry
CV1 5ES

Telephone: 024 7622 7597
E-mail: information@coventrycathedral.org, or www.coventrycathedral.org.

Crafting the cross

A craft idea for making a similar cross

To make a cross of nails of your own, you will need three nails. If you are working with children, you need to ensure that the nails are blunted.

Alternatively, you could use wooden floorboard 'nails', available from a DIY store. These should be glued or bound together with fuse wire in accordance with the design in the picture.

The finished cross could either be sprayed with silver paint or, prior to assembly, the nails could be wrapped tightly in silver foil.

If the cross is to be part of a large display, perhaps one of the following verses (2 Corinthians 5:18–19) could be written nearby, using small paper fasteners or silver drawing-pins to create the letters:

God sent Christ to make peace between himself and us, and he has given us the work of making peace between himself and others.

God was in Christ, offering peace and forgiveness to the people of this world.

God has given us the work of sharing his message about peace.

A holding cross

Bible link: Mark 8:34–35

Jesus then told the crowd and the disciples to come closer, and he said: If any of you want to be my followers, you must forget about yourself. You must take up your cross and follow me. If you want to save your life, you will destroy it. But if you give up your life for me and for the good news, you will save it.

Jesus challenged his followers to 'take up their cross' if they wanted to follow him. It was criminals who literally had to carry their own cross to execution, so these were very troubling words to hear.

Wondering about this Bible story

- I wonder what Jesus really meant?
- I wonder why Jesus said it is so dangerous to try to save one's life?
- I wonder what the crowd made of Jesus' challenge to them?

The story of this cross

A holding cross is designed not so much to look right as to be easy to hold and feel. It is fashioned out of wood (of various colours) with distinctive cross-grains, and then polished. The cross-beam is deliberately uneven or lopsided in its carving, in order to fit between one's fingers more comfortably. Because a holding cross is without decoration or ornamentation or any kind, its look and feel provide a way of remembering the stark harshness of the wood that was used for the cross of Christ.

A holding cross is used in various ways. Sometimes it is simply held in silent meditation or prayer. It can be helpful to hold this cross when saying 'sorry' to God. It also provides an apt focus for praying for others who are suffering. Often it is hard to find words to pray about a situation. In such a context, just holding the cross and picturing the circumstances of that situation can become a prayer in itself.

Here are four short prayers written by Angela Ashwin (from *The Book of 1,000 Prayers*, published by Marshall Pickering). We are grateful to Marshall Pickering for giving us permission to reproduce these prayers in this resource.

In times of distress

As I hang on to this cross, Lord, hang on to me.

Our need for Christ's love and mercy

As I hold this cross, Lord, fill me with your strength and peace.

The cross of Jesus

As I hold this cross, Lord, I remember the cost of your great love for the world.

Resurrection hope

As I hold this cross, Lord, I rejoice in knowing that our evil and sin do not have the last word and that your love is indestructible.

Crafting the cross

A craft idea for making a similar cross

A version of this cross could be made from modelling clay which, when left to harden in the open air, could then be painted to look like wood. Make sure, of course, that you mould the clay to fit your hand most comfortably, rather than trying to make a 'neat' cross shape.

A partnership cross

Bible link: Galatians 3:26–29

All of you are God's children because of your faith in Christ Jesus. And when you were baptized, it was as though you had put on Christ in the same way you put on new clothes. Faith in Christ Jesus is what makes each of you equal with each other, whether you are a Jew or a Greek, a slave or a free person, a man or a woman. So if you belong to Christ, you are now part of Abraham's family, and you will be given what God has promised.

Paul reminded his readers that their newfound faith in Christ cut across all human divisions of culture, colour and class.

Wondering about this Bible story

- I wonder why Paul had to write this to the churches in Galatia?
- I wonder how some of the groups mentioned felt about this part of the letter?
- I wonder what divisions there still are today in the Church?

The story of this cross

The Christian community in the United Kingdom is made up of a great number of church members who worship in different buildings and in a variety of styles. Among these are the churches of the African-Caribbean tradition. Sadly, there is often little contact between black Christians and white congregations. One group that has been trying to encourage links between them is the Centre for Black and White Christian Partnership, which is based in Birmingham.

Its aim is to develop respect and understanding between churches, building bridges of friendship and overcoming some of the fears that exist even between Christians. There is so much to be gained through partnership. Right on our doorstep, links between black and white are a source of encouragement that can help churches in God's mission today.

The centre runs short courses and seminars for church groups and other organizations, at which Christians from different backgrounds can come to a better understanding and appreciation of each other and are encouraged to work together for the kingdom of God in Britain. The centre is also involved in fostering international links with churches and church-related organizations outside the British Isles. In addition, the centre contains a library for information and research.

The centre has produced an educational pack for schools, containing information for teachers about the black-majority churches in Britain as well as a set of full-colour A4 photographs that are designed to stimulate discussion in the classroom.

For further information, contact The Centre for Black and White Christian Partnership, Selly Oak Colleges, Birmingham B29 6LQ; telephone 0121 472 8852.

Most of the black-majority churches in Britain began in the 1940s and 1950s. Sadly, some developed as a result of the racism that their members met in British churches and society at the time. Black church traditions represent many different strands of history, including those that cover the heritage of Christians from Africa and the religious experiences of slaves in the Caribbean and black Pentecostal Christians born in the UK.

Black-majority churches are found in many denominational groupings, including Pentecostal, Methodist and African Independent Churches, such as the Church of Cherubim and Seraphim. They are often well known for their choirs and for worship with a strong emphasis on movement and emotion. Frequently, such worship gives opportunities for everyone in the congregation to be involved in leading prayers or sharing their faith story.

Are there any black-majority church groups in your area? See if you can either arrange a visit to a black-majority church or invite someone from its congregation to come and talk with you.

The Bible is at the heart of all that is done in these churches and, of course, its precepts and teachings are essential to Christians of all denominations. In a black Pentecostal church, for example, there are many opportunities for studying the Bible. Children are encouraged to read it regularly and to learn some important verses off by heart.

Black gospel music is very popular, not only in the church worship of that tradition. Examples of it, using powerful rhythms and heartfelt messages, have often hit the charts. Lively singing is certainly a part of black-majority worship. Many of the 'spirituals' have their roots in the experiences of slavery and pick up the Christian themes of hope and heaven.

Crafting the cross

A craft idea for making a similar cross

The cross in this section is the special logo for the Centre for Black and White Christian Partnership. Why not make your own version of it, using both black and white insulating tape, available from hardware stores, and some short lengths of bamboo cane?

What other designs can your group create that also express partnership between different groups in your church or school?

St Alban's cross

Bible link: John 15:12–17

Now I tell you to love each other, as I have loved you. The greatest way to show love for friends is to die for them. And you are my friends, if you obey me. Servants don't know what their master is doing, and so I don't speak to you as my servants. I speak to you as my friends, and I have told you everything that my Father has told me. You did not choose me. I chose you and sent you out to produce fruit, the kind of fruit that will last. Then my Father will give you whatever you ask for in my name. So I command you to love each other.

Jesus gave his followers the command to love one another. This is a love measured and empowered by the love he demonstrates as he goes to the cross. This love produces results that last.

Wondering about this Bible story

- I wonder whether Jesus' disciples really understood how much Jesus loved them?
- I wonder what makes anyone a friend of Jesus?
- I wonder how giving up life can produce results that last?

The story of this cross

St Alban was the first Christian martyr in Britain. His story is commemorated every year at St Alban's Abbey on Rose Sunday in June. In the abbey there is a window with a stained-glass representation of Alban, carrying his distinctive cross. It has a disc on top of a traditional cross shape containing an icon of the crucifixion, with St John and the Virgin Mary either side of Jesus.

It has been traditional in recent years at St Alban's diocesan festivals for groups to make their own St Alban's cross, decorating it with rose petals around the disc.

In parallel to this first martyrdom in the United Kingdom, June is also the month when Uganda celebrates its first martyrs. In the year 1886, almost fifty young men who were training as priests were burned alive at Namagongo, near the capital Kampala.

A number of churches in the diocese of St Alban's have links with CMS's work in Uganda, and in 2001 the children's festival linked up its Rose Sunday celebrations and its partnership with the worldwide Church, in particular with Uganda. St Alban crosses were made that had a picture of the world in the disc on one side and, on the other, a particular image or symbol linking it with the Church in another country. The festival was called 'St Alban @ the World'.

Crafting the cross

A craft idea for making a similar cross

To make a 'St Alban @ the World' cross, you will need two pieces of wood 150cm and 80cm in length; two circles of card 30cm in diameter; a world template (enlarged and photocopied from the diagram below); coloured paper and other art materials.

- Use stiff card to cut out two circles, each 30cm in diameter.
- Decorate one circle with the map of the world and add the name of your church or school around the edge.
- Design a picture or symbol to decorate the other circle. This could be a symbol from a link that your

group has from around the world, such as the Church in Uganda, a scene from the crucifixion of Jesus, the martyrdom of Alban or the patron saint of a local church, if appropriate.

- The two circles should then be mounted, back to back, on top of the cross made from the 150cm upright and the 80cm crossbeam.
- The upright and the crossbeam could be entwined with coloured paper to match the colours of the national flag of the link country.

St Martin's cross

Bible link: Matthew 25:31–40

When the Son of Man comes in his glory with all his angels, he will sit on his royal throne. The people of all nations will be brought before him, and he will separate them, as shepherds separate their sheep from their goats. He will place the sheep on his right and the goats on his left. Then the king will say to those on his right, 'My father has blessed you! Come and receive the kingdom that was prepared for you before the world was created. When I was hungry, you gave me something to eat, and when I was thirsty, you gave me something to drink. When I was a stranger, you welcomed me, and when I was naked, you gave me clothes to wear. When I was sick, you took care of me, and when I was in jail, you visited me.' Then the ones who pleased the Lord will ask, 'When did we give you something to eat or drink? When did we welcome you as a stranger or give you clothes to wear or visit you while you were sick or in jail?' Then the king will answer, 'Whenever you did it for any of my people, no matter how unimportant they seemed, you did it for me.'

In the parable about the sheep and goats, Jesus told his followers that to care for those in need was how they could best love and serve God. It is on this that the people of all nations will stand or fall on judgment day.

Wondering about this Bible story

- I wonder why people don't find it easy to give things away to those in need?
- I wonder if there's a limit to how much people give away to others?
- I wonder if you know anyone who is always ready to give away or share their belongings?

The story of this cross

St Martin was born in a part of the Roman empire which today lies in Hungary. He was the son of the Roman army officer and spent his childhood in the town of Pavia. His life took a dramatic turn when, in AD337, he encountered a beggar who was freezing cold. Rather than pass him by, Martin tore his coat in two and gave away half to the poor man. Later that night, Christ appeared to Martin in a dream, wearing the half-cloak that Martin had given away. By caring for the person in need, Martin had been serving Jesus, and this was exactly what Jesus himself had said in the Gospels: 'Whenever you did it for any of my people, no matter how unimportant they seemed, you did it for me' (Matthew 25:40).

Martin became recommitted to the Christian faith as a result of this incident and returned to the place of his birth, working as a preacher in his home town. Later he moved to what is now modern France and established the earliest French monastery at a place called Liguge. After ten years he was popularly acclaimed Bishop of Tours (in AD372)

Martin died around the year 400 and soon became a popular saint. Many churches were dedicated to his memory. He was particularly favoured among the early Celtic Church in Britain. Today he is the patron saint of France, and his feast day is 11 November.

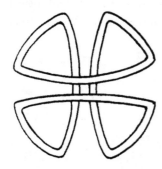

St Martin's Church in Sherwood (Nottingham) uses this cross outline for the saint. The design could be seen in two ways—either as a cross-shaped flower with four petals or an outlined cross stretched across a circle shape, with windows above and below each of the curved arms. Perhaps this could be linked to St Martin's cloak that was used in two ways, as a gift to the poor but also a gift to Christ Jesus.

Crafting the cross

A craft idea for making a similar cross

This activity is linked to St Martin and what his story might say to us today.

Martin himself travelled across Europe and his story quickly spread around the Christian world of his day. The following outline for a talk picks up on the theme of St Martin and the cutting of his coat in two, drawing out lessons about God's worldwide Church and God's mission today. Perhaps your group could present this as a dramatic commentary on St Martin and what the cross meant to him. The Bible links are Matthew 25:31–46 and 1 John 3:11–18.

> You will need six pieces from an old bed sheet, each of them about one metre square.

1. Prepare each piece of sheet to be torn apart easily by cutting a small way into each one at the following points:

   Sheet 1:   anywhere
   Sheet 2:   halfway along
   Sheet 3:   one-third of the way along
   Sheet 4:   one-fifth of the way along
   Sheet 5:   one-tenth of the way along
   Sheet 6:   halfway along

2. Invite some children and adults to come up and help you. Drape the sheets like cloaks around the people at the front.

3. Say, 'What do you do when you get angry? In Bible times there was a particular sign of anger which involved doing something to clothes! Do you know what it was? Tearing your clothes was a dramatic way of showing your feelings!'

   Reassure parents in the congregation that you are not recommending this! Tear the first sheet.

   Say, 'It was used to show anger, and also it was a sign of saying sorry and repentance.'

   Perhaps the group can come up with some biblical examples.

4. Say, 'What else can tearing these sheets show us? It can be a way of sharing what we have.'

   Tell the story of St Martin and ask the next person to tear the sheet in two.

5. Say, 'It can also tell us something about our world today.'

   Have the next sheet torn.

   Say, 'Two thirds of the world is poor and one third is rich. Which part are we in?'

   You could bring in global issues of debt and fair trade here.

   Have the next sheet torn.

6. Say, 'It can also tell us something about the Church. Four-fifths of the worldwide Church—the big family of people who follow Jesus—is not in

Europe, but in Africa, Asia and Latin America. We have much to learn and receive if we are to be like St Martin today.'

Quote some recent example from the mission work of the church.

7. Say, 'It can also give us an idea of what God gives us as a guide about our response to the needs of others.'

Have the next sheet torn.

Say, 'All we have comes from God, but one tenth is for giving back in the service of sharing God's love. He generously allows us to keep more than even St Martin kept!'

8. Say, 'But what is the reason we do this?'

Take the congregation back to the time when Jesus died on the cross.

Say, 'At that moment something dramatic also happened in the heart of the temple.'

Have the final sheet torn.

Say, 'The curtain was torn—a picture of the fact that Jesus has made it possible for us to become God's close friends again, with nothing in the way. We love—and St Martin loved—because God first loved us.'

A Mennonite cross

Bible link: Ephesians 2:14, 16–18

Christ has made peace between Jews and Gentiles, and he has united us by breaking down the wall of hatred that separated us... On the cross Christ did away with our hatred for each other. He also made peace between us and God by uniting Jews and Gentiles in one body. Christ came and preached peace to you Gentiles, who were far from God, and peace to us Jews, who were near God. And because of Christ, all of us can come to the Father by the same Spirit.

Paul writes about the peace that the cross brings—peace with God and peace with each other. This is the peace that Christians are to share with the world.

Wondering about this Bible story

- I wonder what sort of things build a wall of hatred between people?
- I wonder how Jesus and his cross can be the focus of peace for believers?
- I wonder how Christians and others can spread peace in the world?

The story of this cross

On any one Sunday you will find Mennonites gathered for worship in about 61 countries around the world. With over one million members, the Mennonite Church has been in existence for more than 475 years, with a wide variety of practices and people, expressing the one tradition.

It all began in the 16th century when a group of Christians became convinced that they should live more radically and faithfully in obedience to the teachings of Jesus. They were nicknamed 'anabaptists' or 're-baptizers'. They experienced terrible persecution but believed that they should love their enemies as Jesus had done on the cross. They take their name from one of their leaders, a priest called Menno Simons, who travelled throughout the Netherlands spreading the gospel and encouraging other Anabaptists.

The core of Mennonite practice is based on three crucial parts of the Christian story—discipleship (following Jesus), community (submission to God and each other) and peace (love of neighbour).

A Mennonite church in London has expressed its basic aims in a simple way, all linked to the search for peace. Its mission statement, under the title 'seeking to be a peace church', focuses on four key areas:

- **Worship**: the engine of peacemaking, a truthful encounter with the God who loves the world, and a participation in his mission
- **Work**: being peacemakers at work, nurturing peaceful habits, attitudes and skills
- **War and violence**: a commitment to the gospel of grace and peace, reflecting on the scriptures, training in alternative responses, thinking about war and politics and acting for peace

- **Witnessing**: demonstrating the kingdom of God by lifestyle, reflecting on culture, and character training

The Mennonite cross is the chosen symbol of this particular community of believers. It portrays the traditional cross as a dynamic image involving a dove, itself the symbol of peace. The cross seems to be 'on the move', transforming lives and shaking people out of negative and violent lifestyles.

Crafting the cross

A craft idea for making a similar cross

The cross needs to capture both movement and peace in its design. Use the templates below to make a number of crosses and dove shapes, which can then be overlaid as in the picture on page 101.

Different strengths of card and paper, as well as the use of a variety of colours, could suggest the global community of faith and the longing for peace for all nations, which is at the heart of the message of the cross.

A Bible cross

But I will never boast about anything except the cross of our Lord Jesus Christ. Because of his cross, the world is dead as far as I am concerned, and I am dead as far as the world is concerned.

Although the cross was a place of punishment and a shameful death, for Paul it had become his boast and the centre of his new life in Jesus.

Wondering about this Bible story

• I wonder what people at the time thought of Paul's boasting about such an ugly symbol?

• I wonder why Paul felt he needed to boast about the cross?

• I wonder what different reactions people today have to the cross?

The story of this cross

It is not surprising that the cross shape has been picked up in various ways to illustrate Christian posters, artwork or publications. Perhaps the most well-known in recent years is the special 'Good News' Bible cross that is the logo for the Bible translation of that name. This Bible cross is made up of four designs of a head behind an open book, which have been dovetailed together to form the shape of a cross. Can you find any other examples of special cross designs used to illustrate book titles?

There are also many other organizational symbols that incorporate a cross. This often gives a clue to the original Christian foundation of these institutions, even if today the church or faith link is no longer very apparent. Businesses, schools and commercial guilds often have symbols or logos incorporating a cross.

It is interesting to note that the very word 'logo' is from the Greek word *logos*, which means 'word' or 'expression'. At the beginning of John's Gospel, the apostle uses this word to describe Jesus, who is 'God's *logos*'—the one who represents and tells us just what God is like, the living logo by which anyone can recognize God's handiwork. Consequently, it is not at all inappropriate to call the cross the logo of the Christian faith: the cross is the logo of the *logos*, who is Jesus himself!

Crafting the cross

A craft idea for making a similar cross

Design your own cross-shaped logo for a school or a local church. You could even try this with your own name or the name of a group to which you belong.

Make a large version of the 'Good News' cross, putting real faces in the circle shapes. You could use pictures that represent people from different parts of the world. Then put real writing in the book shapes—perhaps from the four Gospels or from four different parts of the Bible or in four different languages.

Other cross logos

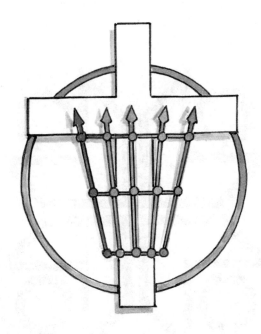

Opposite is a cresset cross from Union Church, Totteridge, north London. This is a good example of a local cross design for a new church building. It is a standard, simple cross set within a circle, but what is striking is that superimposed upon it at its centre is a cresset. This is the name given to a basket-like brazier found in medieval villages, which was always kept burning. It meant that anyone could come there and find warmth or could take from it a flame to light their own family fire.

This is a great image for the work of the people of God—to be a place of warmth and comfort for all people because of the cross of Jesus, and to be a source of inspiration and light that can be taken out into the lives and homes of the community.

Page 158 shows more examples of the ways Christian organizations have used the cross as part of their logo.

PART TWO

Using the crosses
with your group or class

Introduction

This part of the book is a collection of resources that can be drawn upon to meet the needs of a wide range of situations. The materials can be used with children, with adults or with an all-age group. The resources provide material for activity events and workshops, as well as for worship and devotional use both in church and in school. The setting, size and nature of the group, the time and space available and the occasion and purpose of the session will determine which resources are most appropriate.

Much of the material in this section is not specific to one cross. It is general in nature so that you can adapt it to the shape, meaning and story of the particular cross or group of crosses with which you are concerned.

The material is divided into:

- Icebreakers
- Games
- Prayers, poems and quotations
- Craft ideas
- Spoken theme prayers
- Visual prayers
- Key words for the crosses
- Outline for a two-hour programme
- Ideas for a holiday club
- Ideas for all-age worship
- Ideas for collective worship at Key Stages One and Two
- Bible activities for small groups
- Further cross designs and ideas

Icebreakers

The cross is, of course, the symbol of the Christian faith. It is a simple design, and the cross shape in different forms is commonly found in many places.

A useful starting point for an activity on the theme of the cross is to ask a group to identify simple cross shapes in the room around them. As well as sections of window frames or design patterns in fabric, it is surprising how many crosses can be found. As a follow-up, the group could be asked to work together in twos, threes or fours to produce various cross shapes by creating human sculptures. Even the simple act of a handshake can involve a cross.

Drawing on whatever the group comes up with, it would be important to find out what meanings or ideas are associated with the shape of the cross for that particular group. For many today, faith-based or religious understandings will not be the first ideas that come to mind. However, ideas of relationship-building, the connecting of opposites and good luck, which may be expressed by the group, can still be a starting-point to explore Christian meanings for the cross.

Another approach would be to ask for everyday phrases that include the word 'cross'. Each phrase in itself may become another starting-point for a discussion. Phrases that might be suggested include noughts and crosses, cross purposes, cross-examine, cross-eyed, cross your heart, cross your fingers, getting cross.

There are further words which are linked more indirectly to the idea of the cross, such as:

- Crux (as in 'the crux of the matter'. *Crux* is the Latin word for 'cross')
- Critical (linked to the word 'crisis', which is also from the Latin and indicates a point of decision or a crossroads)
- The phrase 'Touch wood' (where the wood in question used to be a 'lucky' piece of the 'original' cross)

The shape of the cross occurs in all sorts of places and can carry a surprising range of meanings. Some crosses form part of the architecture of buildings (often for support, not just decoration) and others are found in statues and sculptures.

Medieval knights, for example, whose tombs can be found in some of our older churches and cathedrals, are usually depicted with their legs crossed in one of three styles. The explanation for this is that it represents the number of crusades in which that knight took part—crossed at the ankles for only one crusade, crossed on the lower leg for two and crossed at the knee for three or more crusades.

During the so-called 'dark ages', the Emperor Charlemagne instituted an interesting legal challenge called 'the judgment of the cross', in which the plaintiff and the accuser in a trial were both required to cross their hands over their hearts. The one who could hold this position the longest won the lawsuit. This may be the origin of the saying 'cross my heart' as a sign of honesty and truth. In a similar vein, the statue of a true knight often had his hands crossed over his heart.

As an introduction to some possible Christian understandings of the cross, here are some ideas for 'living' cross sculptures that could be explored with a group.

GOD'S PEACE

Invite the group to get into threes. Two of the three should play out the role of two antagonists 'at war' with each other, using threatening and angry gestures but with no physical contact. Now instruct the third person to come and put his or her arms around the two 'enemies', in the act of uniting them, or hold out his or her arms between them to keep them apart. The three people should freeze that scene as a human sculpture.

Next, the one-time enemies can leave the sculpture as friends, leaving the 'peacemaker' frozen in the shape that she or he took. These 'peacemakers' will be standing in varying contorted shapes, but each basically as a cross. Christians believe that true peace can only come as we draw near to Jesus, and that the way of all peacemaking must inevitably be cross-shaped (sacrificial, painful and hard work).

Ephesians 2:16

On the cross Christ did away with our hatred for each other. He also made peace between us and God.

Colossians 1:20

And God was pleased… to make peace by sacrificing (Christ's) blood on the cross.

GOD'S LOVE

Invite the group to get into pairs, standing face to face. Ask one person in each pair to stretch up as tall as he or she can go, creating as high a statue as

possible. Then ask the other to stretch out to the side with both hands outstretched, creating as wide a statue as possible. If the two come as close as

possible to each other, the resulting sculpture should be a large cross. Christians believe that the cross is the place where, with others, they can catch a glimpse of how great (how high and how wide) God's love is for humankind—a glimpse that we cannot grasp on our own.

Bible link: Ephesians 3:18–19

I pray that you and all God's people will understand what is called wide or long or high or deep. I want you to know all about Christ's love, although it is too wonderful to be measured.

GOD'S 'YES'

Invite the group, in twos and threes, to create some body sculptures representing letters of the alphabet —A to W. (It can be fun seeing how they interpret a W, S, F, O and B!) Now ask individuals to create a Y and to hold that sculpture position for as long as possible. The shape is like that of a person on a cross, and the 'Y' could stand for several words, such as:

- **Yahweh**: the name God gave for himself to Moses.
- **Yell**: the loud cry of 'It is finished' that Jesus shouted from the cross.
- **Yield**: the willing sacrifice that Jesus offered on behalf of the world.
- **Yes**: Jesus' obedient response to his Father as well as the affirmative welcome the cross can be to all who turn to Jesus.

Bible link: 2 Corinthians 1:20

Christ says 'Yes' to all of God's promises. That's why we have Christ to say 'Amen' for us to the glory of God.

GOD'S HANDPRINT

Teach the group one way to make the 'sign of the cross'. (Refer to the chapter on the Orthodox cross, page 70, for more details.)

- With the right hand, link up thumb and third finger (the one next to the smallest finger)
- With this hand, draw a line from head to heart and then across the body. In the Western tradition the last movement is from left to right and in the Orthodox tradition from right to left.

The cross shape that the group is making is primarily linked to the words 'In the name of the Father and of the Son and of the Holy Spirit'. However, other interpretations could be explored, such as:

- Head, heart, soul and strength
- Thinking, feeling, instincts and energies
- North, south, east and west
- Here, now, in the past and in the future

Can the group think of any more?

In the Orthodox tradition, it is also common to bend low to the ground and draw up the cross shape over the whole body, from bottom to top and right to left. Associated words here could be:

- From death to life
- From self to others
- From grace to glory
- From inside to outside

Christians believe that the sacrificial love expressed by the cross is the real evidence that God is present in any situation. It is like God's fingerprint—unique proof that God is at work. An Orthodox priest once wrote, 'The cross sanctifies the universe.'

Bible link: Colossians 1:17

 God's Son was before all else, and by him everything is held together.

GOD'S FRIENDSHIP

Ask the group to stand in a circle and then to link up with each other, not by holding hands but by resting their arms on the shoulders of their neighbour on either side. This shape is a friendship circle, and it is made up of each person linked to the other in the shape of a cross.

Bible link: Ephesians 2:14

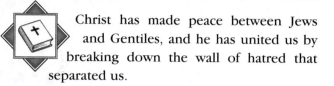 Christ has made peace between Jews and Gentiles, and he has united us by breaking down the wall of hatred that separated us.

GOD'S SUPPORT

Ask the group to work together in threes, in order for two of the group to lift up the third on a seat that they make with their hands. The safest and most secure seat is formed by each of the lifters crossing their hands before holding on to the other's hands. By sitting on this 'cross-seat' and resting his or her arms on the shoulders of those who were lifting, the third person can be safely raised. For safety, ensure that the 'lifters' are not too small to hold the third person. In a similar way, Christians believe that they are raised up by the cross to a new life with Jesus.

Bible link: Romans 6:4

When we were baptized, we died and were buried with Christ. We were baptized, so that we would live a new life, as Christ was raised to life by the glory of God the Father.

Games

THE MESSAGE OF THE CROSS (1)

> You will need cards with suitable words written on them such as joy, hope, love, salvation, peace and forgiveness. Make enough cards for all the children in your group, duplicating the words three or four times depending on the number in the group.

Sit the children in a circle (on chairs preferably) and give each child a card. Make sure that they all know what their word is. Then remove one chair and invite the person whose chair it was to stand in the middle of the circle.

Say, 'The message of the cross is...' (and fill in with one of the words on the cards).

All the children with that word must change seats. The person in the middle also tries to sit down on a spare seat. The person left without a chair after all have moved goes to stand in the middle.

Say again, 'The message of the cross is...' (and complete the sentence with a different word). The game continues until all the children have moved.

THE MESSAGE OF THE CROSS (2)

> You will need some cards as above, but this time showing key words for the crosses, one word on each card. You will find key words on page 129.

Before the game begins, create a series of groupings of these words (three, four or five words at a time depending on the age of the children playing the game), which you will use to complete the statement: 'The message of the cross is...'. For example, you might use 'The message of the cross is... love, forgiveness, unity, peace'.

Give out the cards randomly. The group's task is to arrange themselves into the order as read out by the leader.

You could play against the clock and see how fast the children can get themselves in the correct order.

HAMMER RACE

> For each team you will need a large wooden cross. This can be made simply from two pieces of rough timber. You will also need pieces of card showing each of the key words for the crosses as on page 129. Each team needs a child's hammer and some small nails.

The children stand in their teams at one end of the room. Place the crosses, hammers and nails at the other end. The children run in turn to the cross allocated to their team and nail a card to the cross. The nails must be hammered flat to qualify.

Make sure this activity is well supervised. The winning team is not necessarily the fastest but the one whose cards are most neatly hammered in.

PASS THE BALLOON

Write 'The message of cross is...' on small pieces of paper, filling in the gap with one or more key words from page 129. Insert each piece of paper into the neck of a balloon before inflating the balloons. Use enough balloons for your group to have one per team of three or four players.

Teams have to line up and pass the balloon along the line between their legs. The last person must then run round the line and take up a position at the front to pass the balloon back down the line again. Continue until the team is back in its original order. They then repeat the process, this time passing the balloon along over their heads.

The winning team is the first team to reach their original order with the balloon at the front, burst the balloon and sit down. They then read out the 'message of the cross' that was inside their balloon.

JIGSAW

> You will need pens, thick A4 card and scissors for each team.

Teams are given the task of creating a jigsaw with 24 pieces, which shows the following words in different colours: peace, love, unity, hope, encouragement and victory.

You could choose different sets of six key words for each team, using the list on page 129.

The winning team is the first to finish, having designed, cut and reassembled their jigsaw.

MESSAGES

This game must be played without noise!

Split the children into teams and stand the teams in lines at one end of a room. Each team needs a different message from the following list:

- The message of the cross is love
- Jesus died to set us free
- Jesus died for you and me
- The cross tells us God understands

Each team chooses a message-giver, who runs to the other end of the room where a leader whispers a message to him or her. The message-giver must whisper that message to each new team member when, on a given signal, that member runs to join them from the other end of the room.

The winning team is the team that runs back to its original position and can repeat the correct message when asked. Finish the game by each team in turn shouting their message.

GOOD NEWS

> You will need one set of four cards for each team, showing the words love, peace, hope and unity. You also need sheets of A4 paper, two for each team, with the words 'Good news' written on them.

Divide the group into teams of four. Each team member carries one of the cards (love, peace, hope or unity) and the whole team shares use of the two pieces of A4 paper with the words 'Good news' written on them.

Each team member has to get from one end of the room to the other, carrying their card, only by stepping on the A4 papers. At the opposite end of the room, have pictures of the world where team members can leave their cards.

Their task is to take the good news of love, peace, hope and unity to the world. Each player must return to the team as quickly as possible with the two A4 pieces of papers so that the next team member can begin.

The winning team is the one that finishes first, having delivered all four cards and returned to their original places.

ALPHABET OF CROSSES

> You will need small line drawings of the crosses, photocopied from pages 16–20.

Mark each line drawing with a number (1–40), and place them all around the room. (You do not need to use all 40 crosses; adjust according to the size of your group.)

Give each child or group of children a sequence of numbers (for example, 1, 7, 20, 6, 15). These numbers should correspond to the selection of numbers on the pictures that you have placed around the room. The length of the sequence will depend upon the age of the children and the time available for the game. Each child or team could have a different sequence of numbers.

On the word 'go', the children have to find the cross marked with each number in their sequence, and arrange the crosses, at a given place, in the order of the sequence.

Make sure that you have provided duplicate crosses if the same number is repeated in different sequences.

SHAPES AND MEANINGS

> You will need pictures of crosses photocopied from pages 16–20.

Put the pictures or groups of pictures into the corners and other appropriate spaces in your room. Display one or two large-print lists of the key words with which to associate the crosses (see page 129) at some easily accessible places in the room.

The children should stand in the centre of the room. Call out a key word. The children should run to one of the lists to discover which crosses match the word they have just heard, and then run to a picture of one of those crosses. Set a time limit so that the children have to decide quickly.

For example, for 'faith', run to where the Sudanese, Egyptian or Latin American cross is to be found. For 'hope', run to where the Greek, Maltese, Lebanese, Bangladeshi, Swiss or Sudanese cross is to be found.

To make it more competitive, you could call the last child to arrive at a cross each time 'out'. The winner is then the child who is left in the game the longest.

Prayers, poems and quotations

Because the death of Jesus Christ on a cross is such an important event to Christians, it is not surprising that much has been written about what it means to those who believe. Just as different versions of the cross itself from around the world can enrich our understanding of its symbolism, Christian writers from other countries give new insights into, and inspiration about, the meaning of Good Friday for Christians in the UK. Many of these insights come in the form of prayers.

The following is a selection of quotations, poems and prayers on the theme of the cross and its meaning which, in conjunction with the crosses illustrated in this resource, could be used as part of a presentation, school assembly or act of worship.

*

The cross is the hope of Christians.
The cross is the resurrection of the dead.
The cross is the way of the lost.
The cross is the staff of the lame.
The cross is the guide of the blind.
The cross is the strength of the weak.
The cross is the doctor of the sick.
The cross is the aim of the priests.
The cross is the hope of the hopeless.
The cross is the freedom of the slaves.
The cross is the power of the kings.
The cross is the consolation of the bondmen.
The cross is the source of those who seek water.
The cross is the cloth of the naked.
The cross is the healing of the broken.
The cross is the peace of the church.
We thank you, Father, for the cross.

A TENTH-CENTURY AFRICAN HYMN

*

May the cross be my glory,
The cross of paradise.
May the cross lift me up,
May the cross be the light of dawn,
The door of life,
The good cross,
May the cross be my balm,
May the cross bring me vigour!
Amen

A PRAYER ON THE CROSS OF CHRIST

*

Lord, help us to understand the mystery of your cross. Help us to love the cross, and, Lord, give us guts to embrace it in whatever shape or form it comes.

A PRAYER FROM NICARAGUA

*

O God, nails would not have held your Son to the cross had not love held him there. Make us truly thankful for his great love shown on the cross; and grant that it may fix and steady us in those situations and places which we might most happily desert.

A PRAYER BASED ON WORDS OF CATHERINE OF SIENA (1347–80)

*

O Tree of Calvary
send your roots deep down
into my heart.
Gather together the soil of my heart,
the sands of my fickleness,
the mud of my desires.
Bind them all together,
O Tree of Calvary,
interlace them with your strong roots,
entwine them with the network
of your love.

CHANDRAN DEVANESEN. A PRAYER FROM INDIA, FROM *A PROCESSION OF PRAYERS*, ED. JOHN CARDEN, CONTINUUM, 1998

✴

We implore you, by the memory of your cross hallowed and your most bitter anguish, make us fear you, make us love you, O Christ.

A PRAYER OF ST BRIDGET

✴

On me the Son of God suffered for a time.
Therefore, glorious now, I tower under the heavens
and I am able to heal each one in whom
is fear towards me…
no one who carries within their breast the best
of signs need be overfearful…
for by means of the Cross each soul
who intends to dwell with the Lord
must seek the kingdom in the paths of the earth.

FROM THE OLD ENGLISH POEM 'THE DREAM OF THE ROOD', IN WHICH THE CROSS SPEAKS

✴

May the cross of the Son of God
who is mightier than all the hosts of satan
and more glorious than all the angels of heaven
abide with you in your going out
and your coming in.
By day and by night,
at morning and at evening,
at all times and in all places
may it protect and defend you.

PART OF 'THE CHRISTARAKSHA' FROM *THE PRAYER BOOK OF THE CHURCH OF INDIA*, 1951

✴

When I survey the wondrous cross
on which the Prince of Glory died
My richest gain I count but loss
And pour contempt on all my pride.

Forbid it, Lord, that I should boast
Save in the cross of Christ my God;
All the vain things that charm me most,
I sacrifice them to his blood.

ISAAC WATTS (1674–1748)

✴

I will never boast about anything except the cross of our Lord Jesus Christ. Because of his cross the world is dead as far as I am concerned, and I am dead as far as the world is concerned.

FROM THE WRITINGS OF ST PAUL (GALATIANS 6:14)

✴

If any of you want to be my followers you must forget about yourself. You must take up your cross and follow me.

THE WORDS OF JESUS CHRIST (MATTHEW 16:24)

✴

Keep us in peace, O Christ our God, under the protection of thy holy and venerable Cross; save us from enemies visible and invisible and account us worthy to glorify thee with thanksgiving, with the Father and the Holy Ghost now and ever, world without end.

A BLESSING FROM AMERICA

✴

O Lord, whose holy saints and martyrs in all times and places have endured affliction, suffering and tribulation, by the power of the Holy Cross, the armour of salvation, so likewise, we pray, send your Holy Spirit, the Comforter and Advocate of all Christians, to sustain the churches in their martyrdom, witness and mission.

THE PRAYER OF A ROMANIAN CHRISTIAN

✳

Ave crux, spes unica. ('Hail cross, thou our only hope.')
AN ANCIENT PRAYER

✳

The cross of the Lord protect those who belong to Jesus and strengthen your hearts in faith to Christ in hardship and in ease, in life and in death, now and for ever. Amen
A BLESSING GIVEN BY BISHOP SIMON OF IRAN IN THE FOURTH CENTURY AD

✳

Minister: All our problems
All: **We send to the cross of Christ.**
Minister: All our difficulties
All: **We send to the cross of Christ.**
Minister: All the devil's work
All: **We send to the cross of Christ.**
Minister: All our hopes
All: **We set on the risen Christ.**
FINAL BLESSING, FROM THE KENYAN LITURGY FIRST PUBLISHED IN 1989

These words are usually accompanied by sweeping actions with the arms towards the cross. The whole group is invited to 'act out' the words with these movements.

✳

The cross has won. It always wins!
AN EARLY CHRISTIAN INSCRIPTION FROM THE NUBIAN CHURCH

✳

Across the barriers that divide race from race
Reconcile us, O Christ, by your cross.

Across the barriers that divide the rich from the poor
Reconcile us, O Christ, by your cross.

Across the barriers that divide people of different faiths
Reconcile us, O Christ, by your cross.

Across the barriers that divide Christians
Reconcile us, O Christ, by your cross.

Across the barriers that divide men and women and young and old
Reconcile us, O Christ, by your cross.

✳

My cross is a rainbow-coloured cross,
Violet, indigo, blue, green, yellow, orange, red,
Colours of the rainbow,
A rainbow showed centuries ago to Noah
In a promise never to destroy life again
In a promise fulfilled two thousand years ago,
Redeeming humankind
On the cross.

My cross is a rainbow-coloured cross
To liberate all,
North and south, east and west,
Black and white, yellow and brown,
Male and female.

My cross is a rainbow-coloured cross,
For I am blue with the pain of oppression
And blue with the struggle for freedom
And green with hope.
A PRAYER FROM INDIA, JUDITH SEQUEIRA, © *IN GOD'S IMAGE*

✳

Nothing in my hand I bring,
Simply to thy cross I cling…
Rock of ages, cleft for me,
Let me hide myself in thee.
AUGUSTUS MONTAGUE TOPLADY (1740–78)

✳

May the cross of the Son of God, who is mightier than all the powers of evil, abide with you in your going out and your coming in! From the wrath of evil people, from the temptations of the devil, from all low passions that beguile the soul and body, may it guard, protect and deliver you: and may the blessings of God Almighty, the Father, the Son and the Holy Spirit, be among you and remain with you always. Amen

PRAYER FOR HOLY CROSS DAY (14 SEPTEMBER) FROM *THE BOOK OF COMMON PRAYER* OF THE CHURCH OF INDIA, PAKISTAN, BURMA AND CEYLON, 1978

✳

Crux probat omnia. ('Everything is put to the test by the cross.')

MARTIN LUTHER (1483–1546)

✳

If we have never sought, we seek thee now;
Thine eyes burn through the dark, our only stars;
We must have sight of thorn-marks on thy brow;
We must have thee, O Jesus of the scars.

The other gods were strong; but thou wast weak;
They rode, but thou didst stumble to a throne;
But to our wounds, only God's wounds can speak,
And not a God has wounds, but thou alone.

'JESUS OF THE SCARS' BY EDWARD SHILLITO (1872–1948)

✳

God so loved the world.
See… the love of the Father crucifying
the love of the Son crucified
the love of the Spirit triumphing by the
power of the cross.

METROPOLITAN PHILARET OF MOSCOW (1782–1867)

✳

The king of glory… said, 'All of you come with me, as many as have died through the touch of his hand on the tree; for behold, I raise you all up through the tree of the cross.'

GOSPEL OF NICODEMUS

✳

And I saw a light-filled man emerge from the dawn and pour his brightness over the darkness; it repulsed him; he turned blood-red and pallid, but struck back against the darkness with such force that the man who was lying in the darkness became visible and resplendent through this contact, and standing up, he came forth out of the darkness.

HILDEGARD OF BINGEN (12TH-CENTURY NUN, VISIONARY AND POET)

✳

And the Son of Man was not crucified once for all,
The blood of the martyrs not shed once for all,
The lives of the Saints not given once for all:
But the Son of Man is crucified always
And there shall be Martyrs and Saints.

T.S. ELIOT (1888–1965), CHORUSES FROM 'THE ROCK'

✳

The cross sanctifies the universe.

BISHOP ANASTASIOS (ORTHODOX)

✳

This Holy Mass, this Eucharist, is an act of faith. With Christian faith we know that at this moment the wheaten host is changed into the body of the Lord, who offered himself for the world's redemption, and in this chalice the wine is transformed into the blood that was the price of salvation. May this body… and this blood… nourish us also, so that we may give our body and blood to suffering and to pain—like Christ, not for self, but to teach justice and peace to our people.

THE LAST WORDS OF ARCHBISHOP OSCAR ROMERO BEFORE HE WAS SHOT ON 24 MARCH 1980 TO FALL BEHIND THE ALTAR AT THE FOOT OF A LARGE CRUCIFIX

✴

Lord, save your people
And bless your inheritance,
Granting to faithful Christians
victories over their enemies,
And the protecting of your Commonwealth
by your cross.

ORTHODOX PRAYER FOR THE UNIVERSAL EXULTATION
OF THE PRECIOUS CROSS

✴

How great the cross! What blessings it holds! He who possesses it, possesses a treasure, more noble, more precious than anything on earth.

FROM THE HOMILIES OF ST ANDREW OF CRETE (c.660–740)

✴

You're looking at my wounds, my pain.
I'm looking at yours.
You're looking at the damage to my body.
I'm looking at the damage to yours.
You're thinking of the agony in my heart.
I'm thinking of yours.
You're thinking of the destruction of my hopes.
I'm thinking of the destruction of yours.
You're thinking 'How will he face death?'
I'm thinking 'How will you face yours?'
You say, 'How can God let this happen?'
I say, 'Why shouldn't he? He loves you.'
You say, 'I'm not worth it.'
And that's the difference between us.
You see, I know that you are.

A REFLECTION FROM THE CROSS, IN WHICH JESUS HIMSELF SPEAKS TO HIS
CREATION, BY JIM SMITH, FROM PEOPLE OF THE CROSS (CMS, 2000)

✴

Christ is risen from the dead, trampling down
Death by death
And giving life to those who were in the grave.
We have seen the resurrection of Christ,
So let us bow down before the Holy Lord Jesus,
The only sinless one.
We adore your cross, O Christ,
And we praise and glorify your holy resurrection.

For you are our God, we know no other
apart from you,
And we call on your name.
O come, all you faithful, let us adore
Christ's holy resurrection;
For joy has come into the whole world
through the cross.
Let us sing of his resurrection,
continually blessing the Lord.
He has endured the cross,
destroying Death by death.

A FOCUS ON THE CROSS, USED DURING THE ORTHODOX EASTER LITURGY

✴

At the cross, glorious heaven and wounded earth meet as we catch glimpses of the resurrection. Encountering God at the cross enables suffering and weakness to become opportunities for further humble, compassionate mission.

FROM PEOPLE OF THE CROSS (CMS, 2000)

✴

On Ash Wednesday, in some Christian traditions, the ashes from the burning of last year's palm crosses are used to make the sign of the cross on the forehead of Christians as they begin the season of Lent.

*

I have never seen a battlefield as anything but a crucifix. I have never seen the world as anything but a crucifix.

GEOFFREY STUDDERT KENNEDY (1883–1929), WORLD WAR I ARMY CHAPLAIN. FROM *THE WORD AND THE WORK*, HODDER & STOUGHTON, 1965

*

He opened wide his arms for us on the cross.

FROM THE CHURCH OF ENGLAND'S *COMMON WORSHIP*

*

Be Christ's cross on your new dwelling
Be Christ's cross on your new hearth
Be Christ's cross on your new abode
Upon your new fire blazing.

CELTIC BLESSING FOR A NEW HOME, FROM *CARMINA GADELICA* 111, 367

*

We receive this child into the congregation of Christ's flock, and sign him/her with the sign of the cross, in token that hereafter he/she shall not be ashamed to confess Christ crucified and manfully to fight under his banner against sin, the world and the devil and to continue Christ's servant unto his/her life's end. Amen

THE BAPTISM OF A CHILD, FROM *THE BOOK OF COMMON PRAYER*

*

Tell how Christ, the world's redeemer
As a victim won the day
Amidst the nations God, saith he,
Hath reigned and triumphed from the tree.

VENANTIUS FORTUNATUS (6TH CENTURY)

*

Today, he who hung the earth upon the waters is hung upon the cross.

FROM AN ORTHODOX HYMN FOR GOOD FRIDAY

*

O Lord Jesus Christ, take us to thyself, draw us with cords to the foot of thy cross; for we have no strength to come and we know not the way... under the shadow of thy cross, let us live all the rest of our lives, and there we shall be safe.

ARCHBISHOP FREDERICK TEMPLE (1821–1902)

*

The cross is I crossed out.

ANON

*

The cross! It takes our guilt away;
It holds the fainting spirit up:
It cheers with hope the gloomy day
And sweetens every bitter cup:

It makes the coward spirit brave,
And nerves the feeble arm for fight:
It takes the terror from the grave,
And gilds the bed of death with light:

The balm of life, the cure of woe;
The measure and the pledge of love;
The sinner's refuge here below;
The angels' theme in heaven above.

THOMAS KELLY (1769–1854)

*

O cross, that liftest up my head
I dare not ask to fly from thee
I lay in dust, life's glory dead,
And from the ground there blossoms red
Life that shall endless be.

GEORGE MATHESON (1842–1906)

*

Jesus, cross-bearer,
You carry your people's burden,
And lift from their shoulders the weight of pain.
Jesus, cross-sufferer,

You share your people's anguish,
And bear them through their despair.
Jesus, cross-victor,
You lead your people on,
And bring them to your dawn of hope.

FROM *PRAYERS FOR MISSION 2000* (USPG)

✳

In the cross is salvation, in the cross is life; in the cross is defence from enemies, in the cross heaven's sweetness is outpoured; in the cross is strength of mind; in the cross is joy of spirit; in the cross is highest virtue; in the cross is perfect wholeness. There is no salvation for the soul nor hope of eternal life except in the cross.

'ON THE ROYAL WAY OF THE HOLY CROSS' FROM *THE IMITATION OF CHRIST* BY THOMAS À KEMPIS (c.1380–1471)

✳

We ask you, dear God
That just as the great Southern Cross
Guides our people as they sail
Over the Pacific at night,
So may the cross of Jesus Christ
Lead us through this night
And guide us safely into a new day.

PRAYER FROM PAPUA NEW GUINEA

✳

The cross taught all wood to resound his name
Who bore the same.

FROM 'EASTER', GEORGE HERBERT (1593–1633)

✳

As the emperor Constantine was preparing for battle, he had a dream or vision, in which God sent him a miraculous sign. It was in the afternoon and the sun was setting, when Constantine saw in the sky above the sun a cross, with an inscription which said 'In this sign conquer'. Tradition has it that the sign he saw was the Chi-Rho, which are the first two letters of the Greek word for Christ. The emperor ordered that a replica of this sign be made for

himself and that thereafter this sign should be placed on all the standards of his legions. It was in this sign that Constantine's army went on to be victorious.

✳

By the cross I mean not the wood but the passion. That cross is in Britain, in Ireland, in the whole world. Happy is he who carries in his own heart the cross, the resurrection, the place of the nativity and the ascension.

EPISTLE 58, ST JEROME (c.342–420)

Craft ideas

This is a collection of simple, easily resourced craft ideas. They can be adapted for use with any of the cross designs. They can easily be incorporated into a programme and used to reinforce the teaching about any particular cross and the stories, themes and key words associated with it.

MOBILES

Create mobiles using different sizes of card, with the key words (see page 129) or pictures of the different styles of cross printed on them.

PLAY DOUGH

For this simple recipe you will need:
- ✠ 2 cups flour
- ✠ 1 cup salt
- ✠ 1 tablespoon oil
- ✠ 2 teaspoons cream of tartar
- ✠ 2 cups water
- ✠ Few drops of food colouring

Mix all the ingredients together well. Place in a microwave and heat on the highest setting for two minutes. Stir well. Replace in a microwave for a further two minutes. Turn out and knead the dough until smooth.

BAKING DOUGH OR CLAY

You will need:
- ✠ 4 cups flour
- ✠ 1 cup salt
- ✠ 1 cup hot water

Mix all the ingredients together into a soft dough, and model the dough as desired. Place the finished models on a baking tray and bake in a preheated oven (150°C/300°F/Gas Mark 2) for about two hours. When cooked, the models can be painted or glazed with PVA glue.

You might like to model the shape of the cross in the dough. Make a hole at the top of the cross with a pencil, bake and then paint or glaze the finished piece. The cross, depending on its size, can be either hung on the wall or attached to a cord to wear round the neck.

PRINTING

Any objects can be used to create the required patterns to decorate crosses. You could experiment with corks, bobbins, fingerprints, leaves, vegetables, bottle tops or sponges (cut to shape). Alternatively, there are lots of printing 'stamps' on the market.

Some crosses have very simple patterns and others are very complex. See how many different 'stamps' you can create to print the required patterns.

WAX RESIST

Crosses drawn on white card or paper with a white wax crayon or candle can be painted over (using watery paint) to reveal the shape of the cross.

MONO PRINTS

Brush a thin covering of paint on to the bottom of a tray. Using a finger or a suitable object, draw a picture of the cross required into the paint. Cover the finished design with a piece of paper and rub very gently. Peel back the paper to reveal the design of the cross.

COLLAGE

Any materials can be used to make collage. Materials for a 'feely collage' include paper or card, fabrics, shiny paper, pasta, split peas or lentils. These collages, once completed, look great sprayed with gold or silver paint.

There are also many types of stickers and decorations on the market. The shape of a chosen cross can be created as a 'feely' picture when different textures are used.

RUBBINGS

Cut some card into the desired cross shapes and glue the finished design on to a backing card. Rubbings can then be created by placing sheets of A4 paper over the cut-out card shapes and rubbing over the paper with a wax crayon or soft pencil crayons until the shape is revealed.

GLASS PAINTS

Glass paints and glass paint pens are available from craft or toy shops. Use them on small glasses, glass jars or on acetate to create window patterns and pictures.

Put an acetate sheet over the bold outline of a drawing of a cross. Draw over the shape on the acetate using glass paint liner. Paint inside the shape using glass paints or glass paint markers. The acetate sheets can be stuck on to windows to make 'stained glass window crosses'.

Read the details on the glass paint very carefully. Some paints are made to peel off the base sheet when dry and to stick directly on to the window, leaving the acetate for further use.

TISSUE STAINED GLASS

Tissue glued behind cut-out shapes and designs makes a very good stained-glass effect. This method can be used for many different shapes and designs of cross.

DECORATING BISCUITS

Use decorating icing gel or tubes of decorating icing to create pictures or designs on biscuits. This is particularly suited to creating the shape of the cross and the keywords associated with it.

DRIBBLE OR DROPPER PAINTINGS

Use medicine droppers or let paint drip from a paintbrush to create a pattern. Patterns could represent tears. Mount the desired cross shape on to a large sheet of card that has been decorated using this method. Add the cross's 'key word' (see page 129).

SEWN CROSSES

Photocopy the shape of the cross on to thin card. If necessary, children can draw over the outline shape using a thick marker pen. Then stitch around the shape of the cross, using a tacking stitch. This is most effective when a bright-coloured wool or glittery thread is used.

USING DIFFERENT TYPES OF GLUE

Give each child an outline drawing of a cross. Colour the crosses appropriately. Put PVA glue into a squeezy bottle, such as a shampoo bottle or sauce bottle. (Remember to remove the original label from the bottle and relabel it as 'Glue'.)

Squeeze a trail of glue over the drawn outline of a cross, and lay thick, coloured string or wool on to the gluey trail. This gives a raised outline to the cross, which, when dry, helps children to feel and learn the shape of the cross. A slightly expensive alternative is to use 3-D paint. Squeeze the paint straight from its tubes on to the outline drawing.

Alternatively, squeeze small blobs of neon glue around the outline of the cross. When dry, they will glow in the dark. If the cross is displayed in a child's bedroom, they will be reminded of the cross and its message every time they turn off the light and see the neon glowing.

DOT-TO-DOT

Photocopy the desired cross on to A4 paper. Use liquid paper or white correction ink to cover bits of the lines, so that the effect of a dotted image is achieved. Photocopy the dotted image for each child. Alternatively, enlarge the templates above.

Young children can complete the shape, using it as a dot-to-dot picture. The dotted outline can also be used for a sewing picture, completing the shape by sewing a tacking stitch in each of the spaces.

Spoken theme prayers

COMMUNITY

Lord God, we are taught in your word that your Church is a body. Jesus, our Saviour, we praise you as the head of the body, giving value and purpose to every member and part. We know that no part of your body can say to another, 'I don't need you.' May we never reject or undervalue other people. Help us to value and respect each other with a love that is yours.

Help us to recognize and value each other's gifts so that we may work together in mutual respect, building your Church and the communities in which we live. Help us to follow your example in all that we share. We pray to Jesus, in the power of the Holy Spirit. Amen

ENDURANCE

God our father, your Son Jesus Christ endured pain and insults, torture and death because of his love for you and for the salvation of your world. We remember in gratitude and humility all those who have endured persecution, hostility, torture and death because of their loyalty and love for you and the work you have called them to do. Especially today we remember the courage and endurance of

....

We pray for all who face persecution because of their Christian faith today. Inspire and strengthen them with the gifts of courage, fortitude, endurance and hope. In the power of the Holy Spirit, enable them to overcome the powers and pressures of evil to find peace in you for ever. Amen

FAITH

O Lord God, you are the giver of all good things. We praise you for the gift of faith and for the generations of faithful Christian people who have exercised the gift of faith in the furtherance of your kingdom. Give us that same gift so that, empowered by your Holy Spirit, we may live and work to bring honour and glory to your name, through Jesus Christ our Lord. Amen

HELP

Help us to help each other, Lord. Help us to help those whose need is great, and whose burden is heavy. Make us as ready to receive the help of others as we are to give it. May we both give and receive help in the fellowship of your Son, our Saviour Jesus Christ. Amen

HUMILITY AND SERVICE

O God our heavenly father, your Son Jesus Christ washed his disciples' feet in an act of true humility. Give us the grace to follow that example. Help us to observe and honour the needs of others as we offer ourselves in your service. Free us from the temptation of living under a shadow of false humility, which distorts you and your will. Purify our motivation so that love for you and for your people may guide all that we do. We pray in the name of Jesus who was humble, even to his death on the cross. Amen

ENCOURAGEMENT

Lord Jesus Christ, you saw good in all whom you met. Help us to follow your example, giving value to all and encouraging each other to use the gifts we have been given, to be bold and strong to stand firm when things get tough and to work together for the common good. Amen

EQUALITY

Lord Jesus Christ, you taught us to love and value each other. You broke down barriers of culture and religion, age and gender. You showed us how human ways of

measuring success count for nothing in your sight because with you all are equal. Help us to look beyond colour and culture, status and position to see people as you see them. Give us the will to strive for the equality that belongs to your kingdom alone. Amen

ETERNITY

O God in heaven, the alpha and the omega, your people have used the simple circle as a shape that speaks of your love—a love that has no beginning and no end; a love that binds time and eternity, far and near, past and present, present and future. Help us to know that as we live in time we are part of your eternity. Help us to trust your love in the future, as we have known it in the past. Help us to rejoice with all who have blended the circle and the cross, to bear witness to your Son whose love and forgiveness is the same yesterday, today and for ever, and in whose name we pray. Amen

FORGIVENESS

Lord, because of the cross we are forgiven. We pray for those who do not seek your forgiveness and those who know nothing of it. We pray for ears to be opened to hear the message of your love and forgiveness, and for hearts to be softened and open to receive it. May we, as people of the cross, hold it ever before us as we live in the joy and certainty of sin forgiven. Amen

HOPE

Lord Jesus Christ, in you is our hope. Help us to follow the example of those who have lived with the beacon of hope always alight in their lives. We especially remember the work and witness of the church in .... As your hope has led and inspired them, may it lead and inspire us to keep our eyes fixed on you and on the kingdom in which you dwell today and for ever. Amen

LOVE

We pray to you, Father God, who so loved the world that you sent Jesus to be love here on earth. Thank you for that gift of love, the greatest of all your gifts. We pray for the growth and development of the work and words of your love throughout the world. May it heal divisions, repair damaged lives, and give courage and boldness to people working for you. We rejoice that love knows no boundaries and that it embraces the world as one. Help us to live and work in the light of that love, day by day and for evermore. Amen

MISSION, WITNESS AND DISCIPLESHIP

God our father, your Son Jesus Christ commissioned his disciples to 'go into all the world', taking the good news of your love. We remember with thanksgiving and gratitude all the men and women throughout the world and across the centuries who have obeyed

your word and been faithful in this work. We thank you for their faith and courage, their energy and commitment, their devotion and love. We pray that we may be filled with their zeal. May the longing to share the good news motivate our lives and inspire our words and actions. We pray in the name of our Lord and Saviour, Jesus Christ. Amen

PEACE AND JUSTICE

Leader: In a broken and damaged world
All: **We pray for peace.**
Leader: In a hurting and angry world
All: **We pray for peace.**

Leader: In a dark and disobedient world
All: **We pray for peace.**
Leader: In the name and power of the cross
All: **We pray for peace.**
Leader: In the name of Jesus who died on the cross
All: **We pray for peace.**
Leader: We pray for peace and justice to go hand in hand
All: **We pray for peace and justice to go hand in hand, for Christ's sake. Amen**

RECONCILIATION AND HEALING

Lord Jesus, you went to the cross for the sins of the world. Thank you for the cross and for its power to bring healing and peace. We pray for those countries of the world torn apart by the hatred of war and strife. We pray for enemies to be reconciled, for divisions to be healed and for people to be united in your love. As the arms of the cross stretch to north, south, east and west, we pray for healing and reconciliation in the world you gave your life to save. Amen

SACRIFICE

God our father, your Son Jesus Christ made the one perfect sacrifice upon the cross for the sins of the world. As we know the joy and peace of the forgiveness that his sacrifice brings, help us to live our lives sacrificially, wholeheartedly giving of our riches and sharing our time and energy in the service of your kingdom. We pray in the name of Jesus who gave his life for us. Amen

SHARING

Lord God, creator of the world and of all good things, you have showered your people with gifts. We praise and thank you for your many blessings to us. As we receive so richly from you, give us the grace to give and share the good things of life with others. We pray for people and nations to be released from the grip of greed and selfishness. May the conditions and dilemmas of our neighbours, near and far, open our hearts in generosity and faith for the sake of your Son, our Saviour, Jesus Christ. Amen

UNITY

O God our heavenly father, creator of the world, you made a world full of beauty and harmony, colour and variety, order and pattern. But your people have chosen the ways of ugliness and discord, division and exclusion, disorder and chaos, separating nations and cultures, the east and west, the rich and the poor, and one part of your church from another. We remember with gratitude those who have given their lives to try to recreate unity among your people and especially in your Church. We pray for the power of your Holy Spirit in the values of your kingdom, to bring healing and hope, unity and concord to your Church so that the good news can be proclaimed for the good and enrichment of all. Amen

VICTORY

Leader: Lord Jesus Christ, our Lord and Saviour, when the power of evil is strong

All: **We claim the victory of the cross.**

Leader: When the influence of evil is all around

All: **We claim the victory of the cross.**

Leader: When the attraction of evil invites young and old

All: **We claim the victory of the cross, won by your arms outstretched for us. Give us that victory today and for ever. Amen**

WORSHIP

Lord God, help us to praise and adore you with our whole lives. In what we say and do, may we breathe in time with the rhythm of your will and your ways. Help us to rest in your presence, joining the angels in praise of you. Unite the praises of your people around your throne of grace so that heaven and earth are one in worship. Give words to our lips, and love to our hearts, today and for ever. Amen

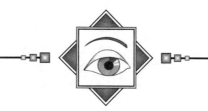

Visual prayers

A visual prayer is a short prayer (like an arrow prayer), which is prompted by a picture or symbol.

Take a small card that is easily held in the palm of the hand. On one side of the card, draw a picture of one of the crosses, and on the other side of the card, write the short phrase or sentence of the arrow prayer. Hold the card in the left hand to look at the picture, and then turn the card over on to the palm of the right hand, so that the words are uppermost. The action of changing the card from one hand to the other is the prompt to offer the prayer.

A visual prayer is suggested in the framework for all-age worship on page 136.

Below is an example of a visual prayer card.

SHORT PHRASES FOR VISUAL PRAYERS

The crosses are listed in the order in which they appear in Part One of this book.

Crosses from Africa

Ethiopian cross: Give us courage to speak out for you.
Sudanese cross: In the darkness, bring light.
Egyptian cross: Bring hope to the homeless.
Mid-African cross: Lord, shine in our darkness.
African crucifix: We pray for good to triumph TODAY.

Crosses from the Middle East

Lebanese cross: Increase my faith.
Palm cross: We praise you as our king.
Iranian cross: Lord, help us to persevere.
Jerusalem cross: Unite us in love.
St Andrew's cross: Send us out in the power of your Spirit.

Crosses from Asia

South Indian cross: Lord, your will, not mine.
North Indian cross: Help me remember you did this for me.
Bangladeshi cross: Open my eyes that I may see.
Pakistani cross: Lord, we want to be fools for you.
Georgian cross: Lord, give me courage.
Asian cross: Lord, you are everything.
Korean cross: We pray for peace.
Chinese cross: Lord, help us and bring healing.
Japanese cross: Help me to cling to the cross.

Crosses from Australasia

Australian cross: Teach us to serve.

Crosses from the Americas

Salvadorean cross: Teach us to love in the way you want.
Latin American cross: Lord, we praise your name.
Peruvian cross: The body of Christ, given for me.

Crosses from Europe

Orthodox cross: Father, forgive.

Celtic cross: Help us to love.

Taizé cross: Lord, make us one.

Irish cross: Help us to give and not to count the cost.

Greek cross: Lord, give them hope.

Finnish cross: Help me to believe.

Maltese cross: Help us to live and work for you.

Roman cross: Great is your faithfulness.

Italian cross: How wonderful are your works, O Lord.

Swiss cross: Love your neighbour as you love yourself.

Cross of nails: Bind us together.

Holding cross: Take up your cross and follow me.

Partnership cross: Lord, make us one.

St Alban's cross: Help me to love.

St Martin's cross: Help us to help each other, Lord.

Mennonite cross: Peace on earth.

Bible cross: Jesus in the centre.

Key words for the crosses

There are many different strands of meaning and experience attached to the cross. In this section we have listed some suggested key words as themes, but from your consideration of each cross you may wish to add many more. Each cross can be studied in its own right or grouped together with other crosses and studied in relation to a uniting theme.

Here are the suggested key words, with a list of the crosses associated with them.

Community
Mennonite cross
Australian cross

Discipleship
Mennonite cross

Encouragement
Irish cross
Partnership cross
Pakistani cross

Endurance
Iranian cross
Ethiopian cross
Pakistani cross
Maltese cross
Chinese cross

Equality
Mid-African cross

Eternity
Celtic cross

Faith
Latin American cross
Sudanese cross
Egyptian cross
Italian cross

Forgiveness
Mid-African cross
Roman cross
Holding cross

Healing
Mid-African cross
Swiss cross

Help
Swiss cross

Hope
Greek cross
Maltese cross
Lebanese cross
Bangladeshi cross
Swiss cross
Sudanese cross

Humility
Georgian cross

Justice
Maltese cross

Love
Irish cross
Asian cross
Bangladeshi cross

Mission and witness
St Andrew's cross
Ethiopian cross
Georgian cross
Egyptian cross
Celtic cross
Jerusalem cross
Irish cross
North Indian cross
Greek cross
Finnish cross
Bible cross
Asian cross
Partnership cross
Chinese cross
Italian cross

Peace
Mennonite cross

Reconciliation
Cross of nails
Mid-African cross

Sacrifice
Salvadorean cross
Palm cross
Roman cross
Holding cross
African crucifix
Japanese cross
St Alban's cross

Service
North Indian cross
Italian cross

Sharing
St Martin's cross
Korean cross

Unity
Partnership cross
South Indian cross
Taizé cross
Jerusalem cross
North Indian cross

Victory
Peruvian cross

Worship
Orthodox cross
Latin American cross
Palm cross

Outlines for a two-hour programme

A two-hour programme is a fast-moving, structured, thematically linked activity programme. It can be planned for children or it can be planned as an all-age event.

This style of working is suitable for groups of any size, provided that the appropriate adult-to-child ratio is maintained. If the group is very small, all the group members can do the same group activity at the same time. If the group is large enough, both or all group activities can run at the same time, and the children can rotate. If the group is very large, there can be more than one group doing the same activity at the same time. For example:

- Ten children or fewer: one group
- Approximately 20 children: two groups of ten, alternating the activities
- Approximately 80 children: eight groups of ten, alternating the activities with four groups doing each of the two activities at the same time

The two-hour programme has a clearly defined aim and content, and the teaching is developed and reinforced through music, crafts and games. Drama and other forms of creative expression can be included if desired.

Balancing the programme

In a two-hour programme, the balance of fast-moving, thematically linked material should be approximately:

- 10 minutes welcome and badges
- 35 minutes on the theme/story/cross
- 40 minutes thematically linked craft activities
- 20 minutes thematically linked games
- 5 minutes refreshments
- 5 minutes closing prayers and reflection
- 5 minutes to collect own things to go home

Total time: 120 minutes

The actual programme runs for 1 hour 55 minutes, with five minutes allowed to collect craft materials and get ready to go home. A timing of less than two hours is suggested because of the Children Act, which states that activities provided for less than six days each year are exempt from registration (and annual inspection), but that the local authority social services department must be informed in advance if you intend to provide any activities that involve care of under-8s for more than two hours, even though registration is not required. Preparation and clearing-up time can be taken in addition. (See page 156 for further details.)

Formal registration of the building and staff by social services is unnecessary for programmes of less than two hours. However, *all* adults working with children must have completed the child protection registration documents required by diocesan or county policy, and all premises and equipment must be maintained in a safe condition. (Contact the Criminal Records Bureau for further information: helpline 0870 9090 844.)

The balance of the contents of the programme is important. The order can, of course, be adjusted to suit the occasion and the creativity of the planning team, but the presentation of the story or theme should not exceed 35 minutes (in total, not at one stretch) because it is reinforced by all the craft activities and the games. To exceed this proportion of time makes the programme feel too heavy.

The craft activities and games should be totally thematically related so that this reinforcement takes place throughout the programme. It is good to have music playing as the children assemble.

It is suggested that badges are made in the shape of 'the cross of the day' or that the cross shape is included on the circle or rectangle that forms the badge.

Sometimes it is possible for the refreshments to have a thematic link, too. For example, at Pentecost you might have flame-shaped biscuits or biscuits decorated with the shape and colour of a flame. A simple cross like that of St Martin or St Andrew can be iced on to a biscuit or a shared cake.

Suggested outline

10 minutes:	Welcome and badges in the shape of…
5 minutes:	Introduction to theme of the cross
20 minutes:	Group activity (craft)
10 minutes:	*Together*: Story expansion of the theme
10 minutes:	Thematically linked game
5 minutes:	Refreshments
20 minutes:	Group activity (craft)
10 minutes:	Game
20 minutes:	*Together*: More about the story/theme with a Bible link
5 minutes:	Closing prayers, quiet reflection, sitting around the shape of the cross that has been the focus of the programme
5 minutes:	Collecting own things to go home

Ten steps to building a two-hour programme

1. Choose the cross or crosses which are to be the focus of the two-hour programme.
2. What is the teaching aim for this programme? Write it down.
3. Look at the suggested outline above and identify the component parts required.
4. Look on the BRF website to find the cross picture(s) for badges for the children to wear, or use the outlines on pages 16–20.
5. Read the information given in Part One of this book about the cross you have chosen. Is there a story that you can use? Are there illustrations that you can show to the group? What is the Bible link? Are you going to use this in the programme?
6. Look at the 'Craft ideas' chapter (pp. 120–122) and adapt ideas to the cross being used. Further craft ideas for the individual crosses are given in Part One.

7. Look at the 'Games' chapter (pp. 110–112) and adapt ideas to the cross being used.
8. Choose music to play as children arrive. Is there a song that fits this theme, that you could incorporate in the programme?
9. Plan the refreshments. Can they have a thematic link?
10. Are you going to use a visual prayer card (see p. 127) or one of the prayers from the 'Spoken theme prayers' chapter (pp. 123–126) in your programme?

Once you have selected all your material and chosen your activities, write up the programme as a timetable and allocate responsibilities to different leaders. Ensure that the programme runs to time and that it keeps moving.

10 minutes:	**Welcome and badges in shape of...** Make badges in the shape of the Taizé cross (create a sheet of shapes from the picture on p. 18 or 73).
5 minutes:	**Introduction to the theme** What does this cross look like? It is shaped in the form of a dove. Why is the cross drawn in this shape?
20 minutes:	**Group activity (craft)** The craft activity is to create many different faces using a 55cm circle. Provide a wide range of materials for the children to use for the craft, such as paints, crayons, collage material and so on. Encourage the children to create 'different' faces—young, old, male, female, different skin tones and so on. Make as many as possible in the time allowed.
10 minutes:	*Together:* **Story expansion of the theme** Sit on the floor, making a Taizé cross shape. Play Taizé music quietly in background. Light some candles (observing safety precautions) and tell the story of Taizé, Brother Roger and the call to unity.
10 minutes:	**Thematically linked game** Split the children into groups and provide each group with a set of 12 plain white cards, each measuring approximately 10cm x 6cm, some pencils, scissors, magazines and glue sticks. Ask the children to write the names of countries from around the world in the middle of the cards (one per card) and glue faces of people around the names (cut from the magazines). Scatter the cards all over the room. Each group has to collect a set of cards to make a worldwide family. Once a full set of 10–12 cards is collected, they have to be arranged in a circle or other formation to show 'unity'. Discuss with the children how they have arranged their pictures to illustrate this quality.
5 minutes:	**Refreshments**
20 minutes:	**Group activity (craft)** Have the bold outline of the Taizé cross drawn as a template. Invite the children to choose from a range of different coloured papers and card, on which they can draw round the template. Cut out the cross, trail glue around the outline shape, and stick thick string or wool on to the glue to accentuate the shape.
10 minutes:	**Game** Make Taizé shaped crosses, one for each child or pair of children. Cut the crosses into ten pieces, and put each set of pieces in a bag or envelope. Give out the bags to the children. On the word 'go', children have to take out the pieces and reassemble the cross. Talk about the crosses being made up from many parts. These represent the *unity* of this cross.
20 minutes:	*Together:* **More about the story/theme with a Bible link** Start with the question 'Who is my neighbour?' Tell the story of the good Samaritan. Everyone is our neighbour: we are all part of one family, the human race created by God. Invite the children to stick the face they made in the first craft activity on to the cross made in the second.
5 minutes:	**Closing prayers and quiet reflection** Invite the children to sit with their cross in front of them. With smaller groups, light a tealight candle and place it on each cross. With larger groups, light a few candles and place them at the front of the group where they can be seen by everyone. Offer prayers for the peace of the world and the unity of its people.
5 minutes:	**Collecting own things to go home**

10 minutes:	**Welcome and badges in shape of...** Make badges featuring a Chinese cross (create a sheet of shapes from the picture on p. 17 or 56).
5 minutes:	**Introduction to the theme** Where is China? Ask the children to put a pin into a map in the place where they think China is. Talk about where China is (show them the correct location on the map if they haven't found it) and say that the cross has incorporated local flower shapes (the lotus flower). Show the cross and the local lotus flower.
20 minutes:	**Group activity (craft)** Start with a basic cross shape and try to incorporate it into the shape of one of our local flowers (such as a rose or daisy). Does this help to make the cross 'your own'?
10 minutes:	*Together:* **Story expansion of the theme** Tell how Chinese Christians have been persecuted for their faith and talk about the growth/persecution pattern. People are still persecuted today. What does the word 'persecution' mean? What do we take for granted?
10 minutes:	**Thematically linked game** Have sets of eleven plastic bottles filled with different amounts of sand (some very little and some a lot). This will make some of the bottles easy and some hard to knock over. Stick letters on the bottles to spell P-E-R-S-E-C-U-T-I-O-N. You need a set of bottles for each group of children. 　　Give each group a supply of soft foam balls. On the word 'go', the children have to throw the balls at the bottles to try to knock them down. Stop in time to talk about what it would feel like to be persecuted in this way, if these bottles were people and the balls were stones or bullets.
5 minutes:	**Refreshments**
20 minutes:	**Group activity (craft)** Give a cardboard cut-out Chinese cross to each child. Ask them to enhance the basic shape by adding the symbols (see p. 57), using glues, glitters and threads. As they are working, ask them for their opinions on whether such additions to the cross enrich or hinder our understanding of it.
10 minutes:	**Game** For each group, cut up a large cardboard Chinese cross into its nine sections—four arms to the cross, four parts to the lotus flower, and the square in the middle. 　　Children take turns to shake dice. They must throw a 5 to put one of the arms on the cross and a 3 to put one of the pieces of the lotus flower in position. When these eight pieces are in place, they must throw a 6 to put the square in the middle. The winning team is the first one to build the cross. If time allows, repeat using different numbers.
20 minutes:	*Together:* **More about the story/theme with a Bible link** Choose one or more stories from the book of Acts, telling of the persecution of Christians in the early Church. For example, you could use Acts 7:54–60 (Stephen is stoned to death), Acts 12:1–5 (Herod causes trouble for the church), or Acts 16:16–25 (Paul and Silas are put in jail).
5 minutes:	**Closing prayers and quiet reflection** Invite the children to sit with their cross in front of them. With smaller groups, light tealight candles and place one on each cross. With larger groups, light a few candles and place them at the front of the group where they can be seen by everyone. Offer prayers for those who are not able to worship freely or who live in fear of persecution.
5 minutes:	**Collecting own things to go home**

Ideas for a holiday club

BEFORE YOU BEGIN

Before you begin planning the theme for your holiday club, check that you have the correct ratio of adults to children, first-aid provision, and that all the helpers are registered through the Criminal Records Bureau (helpline 0870 9090 844) under your church's Child Protection policy. Ensure regular prayer support for the club and think ahead about how you can follow up the event as part of your ongoing work through the church or children's club. See the Appendix on page 156 for further details.

CROSSING CONTINENTS

The different crosses, their stories and the countries they come from open up lots of possibilities for a four- or five-day holiday club theme. One approach is to take the outline for the two-hour programme (see pages 130–133) and work on four or five such programmes as the core material for the club.

Here are some suggestions for activities to include in a five-day club. You will also have ideas of your own to add to the mix.

Choose one cross for each of the five continents of the world as the basis for each day. For example:

- Europe: A Celtic cross
- The Americas: A Latin American cross
- Africa: A Sudanese cross
- Asia: A North Indian cross
- Australasia: An Australian cross

For each location, collect artefacts, pictures and flags to decorate your activity area. As a permanent focus for the club, use a large map of the world on the wall, on which you can plot your holiday club's 'journey' across the globe with large arrows. CMS has large

(1m x 2m) world mats that can be hired for the cost of a donation to the Society's work.

Then create a pattern for each day's activity. It could include the following elements.

Music

As the children come in, play music from the part of the world being featured on that day.

Cultural connections

Give an introduction to the country and continent with reference to details such as customs, language, costume and foods. CMS has a large range of material on many countries, which also includes stories about the Christian family in those parts of the world.

Songs

Choose some favourite songs and choruses that speak of travelling and of God's love reaching out to the whole world. Other songs could link to the particular Bible themes chosen for the day.

Icebreakers

Use some of the icebreakers suggested on pages 107–109 to set the theme for the day.

Bible link

Introduce the Bible story by using the Bible link (see chapters on each cross in Part One). Tell the story using visuals wherever possible and/or invite the children to contribute appropriate sound effects, mime or drama.

The cross for the day

Introduce the cross for that day, with its story.

Craft sessions

Divide the children into groups for craft sessions. Choose craft ideas from the suggestions on pages 120–122 and the 'Crafting the cross' sections for each cross in Part One.

Together time

Come together for a fun quiz on the Bible story and/or a regular daily challenge linked to the culture of that day's part of the world. For example, you could include carrying things on the head (Africa), picking up items with chopsticks (Asia), or learning the steps of a dance (the Americas). If desired, include other games from the suggestions on pages 110–112.

Group time

Get into groups for a session on one of the Bible stories that help us understand what the cross means. For ideas, see the 'Bible links' and 'Wondering questions' sections for each cross in Part One.

Hot seating

If possible, introduce an 'interview' slot with someone who has travelled to or, even better, come from the part of the world on which you are focusing. It is important to try to hear something of the work of Christians today within other cultures. Once again, CMS has contacts with a number of overseas visitors and can often provide stories and pictures for such an interview. It would also be good to learn songs from different parts of the world. CMS has some suggestions of simple world church music that is suitable for children's groups. Further songs could be found among the CDs and cassettes produced by the Wild Goose Worship Group (Iona). Their website address is www.iona.org.uk.

Quiet space

Give the children some space to be quiet, allowing them to respond to what they have heard, using the crosses that have been made. You could use the key words and visual prayers from pages 129 and 127–128.

The story of the cross of Jesus

Make sure that, somewhere in your week, you tell the story of the cross as it appears in the Gospels. This is where the whole message starts!

End-of-week presentation

Invite the children to bring along their parents and carers to a special presentation, when you can share with them some of the stories, fun, crafts and anecdotes from the whole week.

Ideas for all-age worship

THE STRUCTURE OF AN ALL-AGE SERVICE

The service outlined here is structured with the following four sections: preparation, the word, prayers and conclusion. It is suitable for use in all denominations.

The preparation

This section comprises:

- Greeting and words of welcome
- A hymn or song, or opening words with responses
- The prayer for the day (or the Lord's Prayer)

A confession could come after the words of welcome, but in this form of service it is much more likely to come in the prayers as part of our response to the word.

The word

This section includes:

- A reading from scripture: this can be read in parts or dramatized with characters in simple costume and using simple props.
- The talk: this can be very visual, with slides, video, large posters or other visual aids. It can be divided into short sections with activities, music and prayers in between. It can be led by one person or shared between several people. The giving of key words is often helpful for children.
- A hymn or song.
- A declaration of faith.

The prayers

This section comprises:

- Prayers of confession, intercession and thanksgiving, including the Lord's Prayer if not used in the preparation section. Prayers can be visual or interactive in response form
- Prayer processions using symbols can also be used

The conclusion

The service will have some form of ending which may or may not include a hymn or song.

*

The cross being used as the focus for the service could be made from thick card or hardboard in a large format to be carried around the church. It could be carried in at the beginning of the service as a way of introducing the theme, or it could be carried around the church at different points in the service, perhaps during a hymn, to reinforce the theme and help people to identify more with the people of the cross.

The shape of the cross chosen for the service could also be reproduced on small cards. Photocopy the cross shape from pages 16–20, reduced in size so that between 16 and 20 fit on an A4 sheet. A word, thought or simple prayer could be written on the back of each cross shape. These cards can then be used as visual prayer cards (see page 127) during the time of prayer in the service. People might be invited to take them home and continue to use them in their private prayers.

✴

Many of the crosses have stories that are particularly well suited for use at a particular Christian festival, saint's day or other commemoration. Below are suggestions for the matching of a particular cross to a special occasion.

For each date in the calendar linked to a cross, the following details are available from the different sections of the book:

- The story of the cross (see Part One)
- A spoken prayer on the theme (see pages 123–126)
- Suggested reading(s) to develop the theme (see 'Bible links' in Part One)

- Key words associated with the cross of the day (see page 129)
- Ideas for developing the talk (see 'Wondering questions' in Part One)
- Use of a visual prayer (see pages 127–128)

CALENDAR OF DATES AND FESTIVALS WHEN DIFFERENT CROSSES COULD BE USED

The dates and festivals in this calendar are by no means an exhaustive list. You may have other ideas beyond the suggestions below for the crosses that you could use for any particular day or season. The choice is as wide as your imagination.

CALENDAR OF DATES AND FESTIVALS WHEN DIFFERENT CROSSES COULD BE USED

MONTH	Saint's day	Festival or other special day
January	St Anthony of Egypt (17th): An Egyptian cross The conversion of Paul (25th): See key word 'Mission' (p. 129) for a selection of crosses.	Sudan Day (1st): A Sudanese cross Epiphany (6th): See key word 'Worship' (p. 129) for a selection of crosses Week of Prayer for Christian Unity (18th–25th): See key word 'Unity' (p. 129) for a selection of crosses Republic Day in India (26th): A South Indian cross/A North Indian cross
February	St Bridget (1st): An Irish cross	Candlemas (2nd) See key word 'Hope' (p. 129) for a selection of crosses Martyrs' Day in Japan (6th): A Japanese cross Chinese New Year: A Chinese cross
March	St Chad (2nd): A Celtic cross St Patrick (17th): An Irish cross St Cuthbert (20th): A Celtic cross	Pakistan Day (23rd): A Pakistani cross Mothering Sunday: See key word 'Love' (p. 129) for a selection of crosses Lent and Holy Week: See key word 'Sacrifice' (p. 129) for a selection of crosses Oscar Romero (El Salvador) (24th): A Salvadorean cross Bangladesh Day (26th): A Bangladeshi cross
April	Saints, Martyrs and Missionaries of South America (9th): A Latin American cross/A Peruvian cross St George (23rd) See key word 'Mission' (p. 129) for a selection of crosses	Easter. See key words 'Worship', 'Hope' and 'Eternity' (p. 129) for a selection of crosses

Continued on page 138 ▶

MONTH	Saint's day	Festival or other special day
May	Philip and James (1st): See key word 'Mission' (p. 129) for a selection of crosses Matthias (14th): See key word 'Mission' (p. 129) for a selection of crosses St Apolo of the Congo (30th): An African crucifix	Children's Day in Japan (5th): A Japanese cross Ethiopia Day (28th): An Ethiopian cross Pentecost: See key words 'Worship', 'Encouragement' and 'Unity' (p. 129) for a selection of crosses
June	St Columba (9th): A Celtic cross St Alban (22nd): See key word 'Endurance' (p. 129) for a selection of crosses St Peter and St Paul (29th): See key word 'Mission' (p. 129) for a selection of crosses	Martyrs' Day in Uganda (3rd): A Mid-African cross Trinity: See key word 'Worship' (p. 129) for a selection of crosses
July	St Thomas (3rd): See key word 'Faith' (p. 129) for a selection of crosses William Wilberforce, Josephine Butler and all social reformers (29th): See key words 'Discipleship' and 'Justice' (p. 129) for a selection of crosses	Rwanda Day (1st): A Mid-African cross/An African crucifix Egypt Day (23rd): An Egyptian cross Sea Sunday: See key word 'Mission' (p. 129) for a selection of crosses
August	St Aidan (31st): A Celtic cross	Switzerland (1st): A Swiss cross Hiroshima Day (6th): A Japanese cross Holiday club season: See pages 134–135 for a selection of ideas
September	Holy Cross Day (14th): See key word 'Worship' (p. 129) for a selection of crosses	San Salvador Day (15th): A Salvadorean cross
October	St Francis (4th): An Italian cross	China Day (1st): A Chinese cross Iran, National Day (26th): An Iranian cross One World Week: See key word 'Encouragement' (p. 129) for a selection of crosses Week of Prayer for World Peace: A Mennonite cross Harvest: See key word 'Sharing' (p. 129) for a selection of crosses
November	All Saints Day (1st): See key word 'Mission' (p. 129) for a selection of crosses All Souls Day (2nd): See key word 'Mission' (p. 129) for a selection of crosses St Martin (11th): St Martin's cross St Andrew (30th): St Andrew's cross	Remembrance Day (11th): See key word 'Forgiveness' (p. 129) for a selection of crosses Lebanon Independence Day (22nd): A Lebanese cross
December	Saints, Martyrs and Missionaries of Asia (2nd): An Asian cross	Romania Day (1st): A Georgian cross Advent and Christmas: See key word 'Worship' (p. 129) for a selection of crosses

Ideas for collective worship at Key Stages One and Two

At the front of the hall, place a simple wooden cross where it can be seen by all. At either side of it place:

- A picture of the cross which will be the theme of the assembly, as a solid black silhouette or as a simple outline.
- The key word with which the story of this cross is associated, as a black silhouette or a simple outline. The key words for the crosses can be found on page 129.

As the assembly unfolds, these silhouette or outline shapes will be replaced by a more detailed picture of the cross and the letters of the key word. Here is an example of the final tableau:

Many of the crosses presented in this book can be used in this way. The story, shape and key word of the theme could be fitted into this suggested framework.

Key Stage One (15 minutes)

Encourage the children to enter quietly and ask them to look at the table on which the cross and the silhouettes are placed. Draw the children's attention to the shape of the cross in the middle and teach them these words, which could be used on each cross-related assembly.

All: Look at the cross *(put hand above eyes as though looking at a distant horizon)* What do I see? *(draw question mark in the air)* Something that says…

Leader: I wonder what this cross is going to say to us today? We have a cross *(point to the silhouette)* and a key word *(point to the silhouette)* to help us to remember the story of this cross.

Show a picture of your chosen cross and place it over the silhouette briefly, talking about details such as its style, shape and colour. Tell the story of the cross, highlighting the key word which is the summary of its meaning. Cover over the silhouette of the key word with another card on which the letters are brightly coloured.

Where possible, invite the children to draw the outline shape of the cross on the palm of one hand using the forefinger of the other hand. If appropriate, some of the older children can trace the letters of the key word on the other palm, using the forefinger of the other hand.

Having 'drawn' on their hands in this way, invite

the children to 'hold' the story, its people and its meaning in their hands during a short prayer or time of silent reflection. The children sit for prayer with palms upturned.

Choose a short prayer from the selection on pages 113–119, or have a time of silent thinking. After the prayer or silent reflection, choose a song that reflects the theme of the cross. Finally, choose a prayer that reflects the theme, again from the selection on pages 113–119.

At the end of the assembly, encourage the children to leave quietly.

Key Stage Two (20 minutes)

For this style of assembly, it is important to encourage children to enter the assembly hall quietly. Appropriate music can help them to do this. It is good to have a visual focus at the front of the hall on which to concentrate attention.

Preparation

To prepare for this assembly, at the front of the hall make the letters T-H-E C-R-O-S-S into a big, bold display that all can see. The letters could be on a display board or they could be strung together like a mobile. It is important that everyone can see them. Make sure that the letters are well spaced and that there is space underneath to add crosses as the series of assemblies proceeds.

The illustration below shows how the letters may be displayed.

Choose a selection of crosses that could be used for a series of eight assemblies connecting to the letters of the words 'THE CROSS'. For example:

T: The Taizé cross   C: A Celtic cross
H: A holding cross   R: A Roman cross
E: An Ethiopian cross   O: An Orthodox cross
                             S: A Salvadorean cross
                             S: A Swiss cross

Presentation

After an initial greeting and an opening prayer or thought for the day, use the outline for the presentation as given below. The theme of the day is explored in words and with visual support and stimulation. You may wish to begin with a thematically related hymn or song.

For example, songs for the Celtic cross might be:

• God's love is like a circle
• Jesus' love is very wonderful

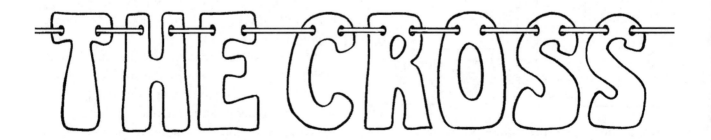

You might choose similar songs that speak of God's love for us.

Every cross has its own particular shape and story. Introduce the shape of the cross for today, for example, a Celtic cross. Show the cross and give its name and the country or countries with which it is associated.

The Celtic cross is particularly associated with Scotland, Ireland and Wales, and is a combination of the cross and a circle. Show this by running a finger round the circle. It speaks to us of eternity. The cross speaks of God's love for us. Together they remind us that God's love is eternal.

Tell the story of the Celtic cross (see pages 71–72), or the story of Celtic saints associated with the cross (see the calendar on pages 137–138). After the story, focus on the cross. Encourage the children to look at the cross and think about its story. After a few minutes, invite the children to watch as you attach the cross to the appropriate letter on the string of letters at the front of the hall. As more crosses are added after subsequent assemblies, the key meanings can be remembered and linked together.

A short time of reflection or prayer might follow. Below is a suggested prayer for you to use if you wish:

Lord we know your love goes on and on for ever. Help us to remember that, to experience it and to share it. Amen

A time of quiet reflection, perhaps including some appropriate music, can follow the prayer, followed by a final song if desired, before the pupils leave the hall quietly.

Bible activities for small groups

Christians believe that the events surrounding the cross at Easter are a defining moment not just for their own faith but also for all people and for all time. The cross shows them what sort of God they believe in and the way that God connects with the big questions about suffering and the meaning of life.

The effect of this one historical Easter event stretches back into the past and forward into the future. The Bible talks of the 'Lamb' (a metaphor for Jesus) who was killed (Revelation 13:8), and a Christ in heaven who still bears the marks of the nails (John 20:27). Christians believe that the cross is there in outline throughout the Old Testament and casts its light forward throughout the New Testament and up to the present day.

The following Bible activity sessions—four from the Old Testament and four from the New Testament —aim to give groups the opportunity to explore why the cross is so central to the Christian faith and what the cross means for Christians today. Each activity has a Bible passage as its starting point, followed by some comments for leaders, some discussion starters and an activity suggestion. These sessions could be used as the teaching element in the programme for a Sunday or midweek group. They could also be used in the classroom as a way to explore how Christians have tried to understand the cross using stories from their special book.

This chapter ends with two activities for prayer and meditation based on the cross. They could be used in conjunction with the sessions below or stand alone as an element in a worship service. In the classroom they could form the basis of material for an assembly or circle time discussion. The two activities are 'A window cross' and 'Touching the cross' (see pp. 150–152).

Old Testament stories

1. The sacrificial lamb: Exodus 12:21–28
2. The scapegoat: Leviticus 16:20–22
3. The serpent pole: Numbers 21:4–9
4. The sign of Jonah: Jonah 2 and Matthew 12:38–41

New Testament stories

1. Peter gets it wrong: Mark 8:31–35
2. Jesus tells a special story: Mark 12:1–12
3. Simon is forced to help: Mark 15:21–22
4. Paul sums it up: Galatians 6:11–16

Christians believe that God's way is cross-shaped. God deals with suffering, sin and selfishness not by magically removing it or overlooking it, but by entering into it. The cross is therefore God's unique fingerprint in this world and the ultimate test of whether something really is God's work or not.

Christians are people whose lives are centred on the truth of the cross, which, they believe, is good news for the entire world. The way of the cross is usually the unexpected, the unwanted and the unworldly choice in life—as Jesus recognized in his comment to Peter in Mark 8:33. It is a choice that characterizes the God of the Christian faith, whose nature is cross-shaped.

Christians believe that the cross is the secret key to the purpose of the universe and the meaning of life. It is the meeting place of time and eternity—the crossroads of earth and heaven, life and eternal life, past and present and ourselves and God.

The following stories explore the clues to all this as they are found throughout the Bible.

The sacrificial lamb

Bible story

Read Exodus 12:21–28.

Comments

According to the Gospel accounts, Jesus' death on the cross occurred at the same time as the killing of the lambs for Passover. God's instructions to Moses for the people of Israel had been that an innocent lamb should be killed and eaten on the night when the angel of death was to 'pass over' the homes of all who were in Egypt at that time. As long as the blood of that innocent lamb was daubed on the posts and lintels of their doors, then the angel of death would indeed pass over and the firstborn there would not die. This was the final tragic plague that persuaded Pharaoh to let the Hebrew people go.

The Jewish people still commemorate this event every year, and Christians see it as one of those Old Testament clues to the meaning of the cross. The poor lamb had to die, and its blood around the door was the sign that saved the Hebrews and won them freedom from slavery. In the same way, Christians believe that Jesus' innocent death means they can be saved from eternal death and can win the freedom of new eternal life with God, which starts here and now.

Discussion starters

• Why do you think the angel of death passed over the homes of the Hebrews?
• Why was it so important to the Hebrews to go on celebrating the Passover, and why is it still important for Jewish people today?
• What was so special about the lamb that was killed?
• What similarities can you see between the Passover story and the events of Good Friday?

Activity

One way to make this story visual is to create a doorway with five pieces of brown card, two either side to form the uprights (all the same length) and one across the top for the lintel (slightly longer). Attach them loosely on to a contrasting background. As you tell the Exodus story, add three red marks to represent the blood, one at the centre of the lintel and one either side on the upper of the two pieces that make the doorposts.

Link this to what happened to Jesus on the cross by rearranging the five pieces to make a cross shape (the lintel becomes the upper part of the downpost of the cross and the two doorposts with red stains become the arms of the cross; the other pieces complete the cross downwards). The red 'blood' stains now show where Christ's head and hands would have been and make the connection between Jesus and the lamb that was killed.

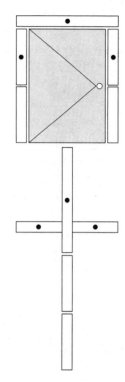

✳

The scapegoat

Bible story

Read Leviticus 16:20–22.

Comments

The phrase 'to become a scapegoat' comes from the ritual described in the Leviticus story.

The people of God had been given very careful instructions about how they should 'get rid' of their sins. God was perfect and holy, so there had to be a way that sinful human beings could be 'cleaned up' so that they could enjoy God's closeness and love, whenever they messed things up. Moses and Aaron established a pattern of sacrifices and special rituals during the time the people were in the desert, after their escape from Egypt. The final and most important way of 'getting rid' of their sins was demonstrated when Aaron symbolically carried all the people's sins and laid them on to a goat, which was then driven away from the camp. It was a powerful visual aid of the people's sins being put on to something else and being taken out of their sight.

Discussion starters

• Talk about what it means to be a scapegoat or to make someone a scapegoat for something that has gone wrong.

• Why do you think the Hebrews needed this ritual as described in the reading?

• In what way do you think Jesus could be seen as a sort of scapegoat?

• Another set of verses from the Old Testament is connected to this whole theme, and Christians find them especially important. Look them up in Isaiah 53:4–6. Why do you think Christians use this reading at Easter time? There are further verses in this chapter that seem to link to the cross. Can you find them?

Activity

As a visual aid for this story, use the famous picture of the scapegoat painted by Holman Hunt. A copy is available to be viewed and downloaded at: www.victorianweb.org/painting/whh/replete/P3.html

• What reactions does the group have to this picture?

• What do you think the artist is trying to say in the picture?

• Do you think there is any way that the artist has tried to make a connection with the story of Jesus?

• The experience of having to take the blame for someone else's mistake or crime is hard to describe. Has Holman Hunt managed to capture it in this painting?

• Can you think of any modern-day groups that feel that they have become scapegoats by being blamed for something that isn't their fault?

In the drawing of this same picture on page 144, create a collage of names, newspaper stories or other pictures or photographs that are connected with the idea of becoming a scapegoat. Do you think that Christians would place a picture of Jesus within such an outline?

*

The serpent pole

Bible story

Read Numbers 21:4–9.

Comments

At first sight, this incident seems to have nothing to do with the cross. The people have given up trusting in God's leading, and as a result a plague of snakes threatens to destroy them all. Moses pleads with God for mercy and he is given the instruction to create a bronze serpent on a pole. If the people look toward this pole in obedience to God's words through Moses, they will be healed. The choice is theirs.

Look up what Jesus says about this story in John 3:13–15 from the New Testament.

Discussion starters

Read the story with your group, using the following retelling.

We were on the march again, travelling south this time, when it all blew up. It wasn't surprising really that our mood turned ugly. We were all fed up with travelling, fighting, camping for a while and then moving on again—always moving.

It would be enough to break anybody's spirits. But now this marching south in order to go north—this was sheer madness. We didn't care whether they were God's orders or not, it just didn't make sense.

Taking the short route would have meant going through enemy territory, but we'd done that before and survived, so why not again? But no, the divine orders came and, grumbling, we set out. As I said, the mood was turning ugly.

There were those among us who remembered walking this very same route before, many years ago, during our seemingly endless trekking back and forth across the deserts from water hole to water hole. To double back on yourself once is bad enough, but it had happened too many times now to be laughed off as a mistake. It was bad leadership; it was poor planning. It was all a disastrous folly—a madness that must stop.

I don't know who first spread the idea, but once the thought was out, there was no stopping it. Everywhere people took up the words: 'Who cares about a promised land? We're not living our life in the hope of some distant paradise, some heaven on earth. We want our own place here and now. We've had enough of wandering the desert roads; enough of sand in our clothes, our hair and our eyes; enough of thirsty days and cold nights; enough of manna to eat in the morning—we want some real bread again. We've had all we can take of Moses and his commandments from God, all we can take of being a special people loved by God. What sort of God lets us wander around like this, year after weary year?'

The complaints grew louder and more insistent. Some groups began to refuse to continue the journey; others besieged Moses, bending his ear with their grievances, their frustrations and anger. Then a new idea caught our imagination. Why not head back to Egypt? We were going in that direction anyway now, so why not? There was water there, plenty of food—and salad and greens and fruit, things we hadn't eaten for as long as we could remember. Some of our youngsters didn't even know what they tasted like. Yes, let's go back to Egypt. Let's give up searching for a promised land. Who needs it? We want full stomachs, not pie-in-the-sky promises.

No one mentioned the slavery in all this.

Egypt meant slavery, but that was conveniently forgotten—logic and sound memories suffer when emotions take control; no one remembered the slavery.

It was then that the horror struck. The first we knew of the disaster was a scream from one of the tents near the outskirts of the camp, towards dusk. And it wasn't the last scream we heard that night. Serpents, small desert snakes, were moving like lightning across the desert, defying capture but leaving a trail of death and pain wherever they had been. They were vipers whose deadly bite injected a stinging poison that burned through the body like a hot needle in every vein and artery.

Suddenly all the complaining was forgotten; all the anger and rebellion died away as we struggled to tend the sick and dying as well as trying to avoid stepping on and disturbing one of our evil guests. And they were everywhere —in our bedding, our food supplies, under stones and by the campfire. We were in the grip of a plague—eating away at our resolve, gnawing at our consciences and leaving a painful reminder that we were so vulnerable and so very human and that death comes when we least expect it.

It turned many of us to prayer and to the God against whom we had been rebelling— the God we Israelites should have trusted. He hadn't let us down yet, despite the long and twisted journey. He'd given us enough to eat and drink. We had been so foolish to rebel, to think we knew better, to prefer Egyptian slavery to freedom in the land of Canaan, God's promised land.

Prayer had always shown us the way forward. So it was to Moses we turned, not now in anger but in sorrow. What could we do? How could we survive the serpent's sting, this poison of death all about us? Moses, too, now prayed and God showed him what to do.

The blacksmith's fire was heated to its maximum temperature. The bronze rod was forged and around it was shaped the curling form of a serpent, also made of bronze. It was a symbol in metal of the very evil that was killing us all—a sign of death hoisted high on a pole, a picture of death itself being put to death. Poles and posts like that were used to execute criminals. How strange that God should tell us to do this—perhaps he had some lesson in mind?

When the metal had cooled, Moses lifted high this symbol of evil punishment and told us all to look at it—even those who were still burning in agony from the bites. We would be well; we would be healed—and we were.

No one will ever forget the lesson of that day—the day of the serpents in the wilderness; the day the bronze serpent was lifted up. Just one look towards it was healing to us, and a new start and a sign of God's patient love toward us, his rebellious children.

Now ask the question:

- Why do you think Jesus used this story to give a clue to the meaning of the cross?

Activity

You will need the following to make a model of the serpent on a pole.

✳ A piece of orange Plasticine or modelling clay for each child in your group
✳ A garden cane 30cm in length (one per child)
✳ Sticky tape

1. Roll the Plasticine or modelling clay into a long snake shape, 12cm in length.
2. Twist the 'snake' around the cane, attaching it with some sticky tape.
3. Pinch the head end and add eye-like markings.

The sign of Jonah

Bible story

Read the whole story of Jonah in the Old Testament—it is only four short chapters!

Comments

Jonah was a reluctant missionary who didn't want to be the one to give a second chance to the people of Nineveh—Israel's cruel and ungodly neighbours.

Foolishly, Jonah thinks he can run away from God. The storm at sea soon leads the sailors to realize that someone on board has brought them bad luck. Once Jonah has been thrown overboard, the storm is stilled and the sailors are safe. Jonah meanwhile is also miraculously safe inside the great fish from where he prays and has a rethink about his calling from God. He does go to Nineveh and the people there do mend their ways—something that Jonah feared would happen. He finds it hard to accept that these 'outsiders' can be forgiven. God's generosity is more than he can stand!

Discussion starters

From the New Testament, read Matthew 12:38–41.

- How does Jesus explain that the story of Jonah is a clue to the events of the first Easter?
- Why does Jesus remind his listeners that the people of Nineveh eventually did pay attention to Jonah?
- Despite the miracles he performed, Jesus also recognizes that people might not believe. Read what he says about this in Luke 16:19–31.

Activity

A suggested outline for a group presentation on the whole of Jonah could take the structure of using different coloured cloths. For example:

- A piece of sail cloth (Jonah on the run)
- A long piece of blue cloth (the storm at sea)

- A piece of purple or red cloth (preaching to the wealthy king and his subjects)
- A piece of sack cloth (Nineveh repents)
- A piece of green cloth (Jonah beneath his plant with his thoughts and God's words)

Finish by linking the story to Jesus' words about how this points to the cross and how Christians respond to it. The connection could be made by using another piece of cloth to represent Jesus' robe, torn and gambled over by the soldiers at the foot of the cross and the piece of linen cloth lying in the empty tomb.

✶

NEW TESTAMENT STORIES

Peter gets it wrong!

Bible story

Read Mark 8:31–35.

Comments

As if to emphasize the centrality of the cross for all Christian thinking, the Gospel writer, Mark, hinges his story of Jesus on the acceptance or rejection of the way of the cross. In Mark 8:34 he tells how Jesus said, 'If any of you want to be my followers, you must forget about yourself. You must take up your cross and follow me.' Of all the teaching about God's kingdom that Jesus had given to his disciples and demonstrated to them through his miracles up until then, this challenge comes as the most important and most difficult truth to accept. There has to be a cross. For Peter (and the others) this is a crossroads and a crisis point. Would they be on the side of God or of the world, as Jesus said to Peter? Would they follow Satan or the Saviour? God's plan for the world and for each person involves a cross, because with God, Christians believe, there is no other way.

No wonder Peter found it hard to stomach. How could Jesus, at the height of his popularity—at the very moment when he clearly had his enemies tongue-tied and beaten—talk about the way of weakness, defeat and death? In human terms, this was to lose the plot, to make a wrong choice and to throw away all that had been gained so far. Peter just couldn't understand what Jesus was saying.

Discussion starters

• How do you think Peter felt when Jesus rounded on him so sharply? (See verse 33.)

• Why was it so hard for Peter and the others to accept Jesus' talk about having to die?

• What do you think Jesus means when he says that his followers must 'take up their cross'?

• Many people today, including those of other faith traditions, also find it hard to believe that Jesus could only be a real king by dying. Ask someone to come and try to explain this to you from his or her own experience of being a Christian.

Activity

This episode is full of emotion. Divide the children up into three groups and work on presenting three snapshots of what happened at Caesarea Philippi:

• The moment when Jesus says that he has to die (v. 31).

• Then the moment when Jesus has to tell Peter off for what he has just said (v. 33).

• Finally, the moment when Jesus tells them all that they must take up their own crosses (v. 34).

Freeze the action each time, with plenty of emotion in faces and the way people are standing.

*

Jesus tells a special story

Bible story

Read Mark 12:1–12

Comments

This parable struck home, and the scribes and Pharisees who heard it had no doubt that it was directed at them.

The vineyard was a way of describing the people of God, so the owner is God, who keeps sending his messengers to bring his people back to the experience of the Creator's friendship and love. In the parable, the tenants decide that they don't need the owner any more and mistreat all those who come in the owner's name. Finally the owner's son comes.

There can be no doubt that Jesus was referring to himself as God's son, and his listeners knew it. He is rejected like an unwanted stone on a building site. However, Jesus turns the story round and, using a verse from the Old Testament, warns his listeners that this rejected stone will become the stone that is used to hold the whole building together. The rejected stone, and the eventual honoured position for that stone, point forward to the Easter story to come.

Discussion starters

• Why do you think Jesus had to use a parable to tell his listeners about what was going to happen? Why not tell them more plainly?

• Why do you think the scribes and Pharisees were so angry?

• Do you think that there may be a note of sadness in Jesus' voice as he tells this story? Do you think he hopes that they might, even at this stage, change their minds about him?

• Which are the clues to the meaning of the cross for Christians in this story?

Activity

Retell the story with two narrators, while the rest of the group mimes the actions.

It is likely that Jesus told this story close to the temple in Jerusalem, which had not long been rebuilt. Perhaps there were still some signs of the rebuilding around—maybe loose and rejected building material, for example. Using some building bricks from a young child's toy set, tell this part of the story by building a doorway. Finish the sequence by using one of the pieces you have rejected to become the key piece that completes the structure. This might in turn inspire some artwork from the rest of the group, picking up on this imagery. It represents another clue to the meaning of Easter for Christians.

*

Simon is forced to help

Bible story

Read Mark 15:21–22

Comments

This is the first reference in the New Testament to a person from the continent of Africa, and it occurs at the heart of the Easter story. Cyrene is in north Africa. Simon was probably in Jerusalem for the Passover celebrations when he suddenly found himself centre-stage, carrying Jesus' cross. Jesus has become too weak to carry the cross-piece to the execution place, so the guards commandeer this outsider to do it for him.

Discussion starters

• How do you think Simon felt at being given this sad task to perform?

• I wonder why the guards chose Simon to help Jesus?

• Mark mentions Simon's children's names. How does he know them, do you think?

• What does his knowledge of them suggest to you?

• Jesus had already said earlier in this Gospel that all Christians, like Simon, are called to carry a cross and follow Jesus. But what do you think this really means for followers of Jesus today?

Activity

How might Simon have written about the events of that first Good Friday when he thought about them afterwards?

Imagine that Simon is writing to his two sons back home about that weekend. You could decide to stay with his feelings as they were just on that Friday, or you could include the rumours and stories about what happened on Easter Sunday morning. Simon may have already heard about Jesus in some way, and that may have been why he joined the crowds on the road to Golgotha.

Begin:

Dearest Alex and Rufus

I hardly know how to tell you what happened to me the other day during the festival here in Jerusalem. It was so terrible and strange…

*

Paul sums it up

Bible story

Read Galatians 6:11–16. The key sentences are in verse 14.

Comments

Paul would once have been among those scribes and Pharisees who had no time for Jesus' talk about being God's son who had to die. This sort of message was complete nonsense to the Jews, as much as it was to outsiders (look up 1 Corinthians 1:18 and 23). But remarkably, Paul (or Saul, as he was known when he first appeared on the scene) had a complete change of mind.

He had come to believe that Jesus' death was the only way that the great gap between sinful humans and a holy God could be bridged. He had put together all the clues in the Old Testament—such as those in this section—and realized that the cross was the key to the whole mystery. He now wanted to talk of nothing else. All that once had been his pride, such as his Jewish identity and heritage (symbolized by the sign of circumcision) faded into nothing compared to a new sign—the sign of the cross. It had changed his world and given him a brand new start—a sort of second creation (see v. 15)!

Discussion starters

- What gives you the impression in these verses that the cross means so much to Paul?
- It took a lot for Paul to have such a great change of mind about the cross. What had happened? See Paul's story in Acts 9:1–18.
- The cross isn't just an event from the past, but seems to do something in the present too for Paul. Read verse 14 again. What do you think he means?

Activity

For Christians, the cross comes to stand as a symbol of the moment when they start to see things differently—including God, themselves and the world. It is a great turning point.

Paul wrote about this in his letter to the church in Philippi (see Philippians 3:3–11). On an A4 piece of paper (landscape), draw a large cross in the middle. On one side list all the things Paul says he counts as nothing, and on the other side all the things that he now thinks are more important.

Not all Christians would have such a dramatic change to talk about. Interview someone you know who is a Christian and find out what changes there have been in their lives. What would their cross picture look like?

✳

TWO PRAYER MEDITATIONS ON THE CROSS FOR SMALL GROUPS

A window cross

Like an icon, the cross can act as a window for Christians, through which they can look at both God's love and God's world. The Bible writers in the New Testament interpreted the cross and its meaning using various ideas drawn from their experience of life at that time.

- The cross was the cost that God paid to buy them out of slavery, just as slaves used to be purchased in the marketplace.
- The cross was the place where an innocent victim was sacrificed to deal with all the sin that otherwise would get in the way between imperfect human beings and a perfect God, just as, in the temple, the sacrifice of a lamb covered the people's sins according to Jewish ritual.

- The cross was the place where the 'guilty' verdict against the world was turned into a 'not guilty', because Jesus took the place of the human race in the dock—to use an image borrowed from the law courts.
- The cross was the place of victory over evil, as pure innocent love alone disarmed the worst that evil could do to it. Here the image is of the battlefield followed by the triumphant procession, which is the resurrection.

All these insights can be helpful to Christians as they try to understand the meaning of the cross. In the end, however, most Christians would admit that what was happening at Calvary two thousand years ago remains a mystery too great for human minds to grasp. The cross is central to the Christian faith and is a window through which Christians try to understand the world and what is happening around them. The following simple prayer meditation picks up this idea as it creates a window cross.

Activity

Fold an A4 sheet of paper in half and then in half again at right angles to the first fold. Cut or tear out an L-shape along the folded edges (the shaded area on the diagram below), and unfold the paper to give a cross-shaped window.

Now, instead of looking at the cross, you are able to look through the cross.

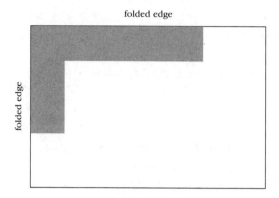

folded edge

folded edge

As a group, think how the world, your local community, the different people you know and the different life experiences you have had now appear, through the cross.

Give space for prayer and some silent meditation as each person turns his or her cross to look at various people, views or (in the mind's eye) situations 'through the cross'.

Christians believe that the vertical (Godward) relationship is as important as the horizontal (human) relationship. The cross shape is a reminder that there is a spiritual dimension to all we see. The cross window also reminds Christians that they can look for God's love in all places and that God's sacrificial love is his 'fingerprint' on the world.

*

Touching the cross

On the floor of the room where you meet, mark with masking tape the outline of a very large cross with equal arms. It should be big enough to enable a group of up to five children and a leader to sit in a circle in each of the arms of the cross.

Now choose four different crosses from this book, which you need to place in the four arms of the cross. For the crosses, you could download pictures from the BRF website accompanying this resource or photocopy and enlarge the pictures from pages 16–20 of the book. It would be best, however, to have real three-dimensional crosses. You may have a collection yourself or be able to borrow some by asking friends at school or church. Many cathedral bookshops carry stocks of different wooden crosses.

If possible, set the picture of the cross or the cross itself within a frame or on a simple stand so that it can be the focus for the prayer activity in that part of the cross marked out on the floor. Alongside each of the four crosses, print out the key words and the visual prayers that connect with the crosses as listed on pages 127 and 129. You could also include a copy of the Bible link written out in full, along with the wondering questions from Part One of this book.

Begin the prayer meditation by explaining clearly what the group will be doing.

1. In groups of six (five children plus one adult), everyone should walk in single file around the outside shape of the cross on the floor and complete one full circuit. As the group walks, you might like to use a simple chant such as the one below, where each line is chanted first by the leader and then repeated by everyone. Try to give it a walking or marching rhythm:

We're on a cross-shaped journey
To touch and see and know.
Around the world and then back home
And praying as we go.

2. Having competed one circuit, each group should then walk to one of the arms of the cross and settle in a circle around the picture or cross that is there.

3. In silence, the group should first of all pass the cross or its picture around the group so that all can have a closer view. The leader could read a short piece about the cross and where it is from, taken from the information in Part One.

4. Now place the cross back on its stand or in its frame and invite the group to pick up the printed copies of the key words, visual prayers and Bible texts linked to that cross.

5. Give the group a set time to read, pray and think through these words. You may also like to provide colours, pencils and paper in case some in the

group would like to pray their thoughts in the form of a picture or write something. If you do this, build in more time for this activity at each prayer-station around the cross.

6. At a given signal, the groups should stand and return to the outside perimeter of the cross and once again walk around a complete circuit, possibly using the chant (see above), before proceeding to another cross focus for the next prayer activity.

7. Continue this until each group has been to each of the prayer-stations.

8. When the groups have spent time at all the cross prayer-stations, the final walk around the cross should end with everyone standing on the perimeter of the cross shape and facing inward.

9. The final prayer or meditation should focus on a central cross for everyone. For this cross, use one that has special local significance, linked to the school, the church or area where the activity is taking place. Similarly, link any activity here to particular local prayers, thoughts and concerns, which could be written out on card and read by members of the group.

10. Finish the prayer meditation with the following prayer, said by everyone:

The cross we have walked
Reaches out to all corners of the world.

The cross where we stand
Points to all parts of our town/city.

The cross where we have prayed
Touches all the people we know.

May the power of this cross strengthen us all.

May the love of the cross renew us all.

May the truths of this cross help us serve God better.

We pray this prayer in the shape of
the cross of Jesus.
Amen

Further cross designs and ideas

There are many varieties of cross designs used by different Christian groups or organizations. Some have links with a particular saint or Christian tradition. Others have a French designation, arising from the use of such crosses in heraldry. Below are the words used to describe examples of these crosses, together with illustrations of their designs.

Aiguisée

Avellane

Barbée

Canterbury

Cercelée

Cross crosslet

Entrailed

Fleurée

Globical

Iona

Millvine

Papal
(The beams signified the
Pope's position as chief
priest, teacher and shepherd)

Patée

Patée formée

Patonce

Pommel

Potent

St Andrew's
(a white cross on a blue
background)

or St Patrick's (red)

or St Alban's (gold)

or St Osmund's (blue)

Raguly

St Peter's

Tau (St Anthony's)

Trefly

Huguenot

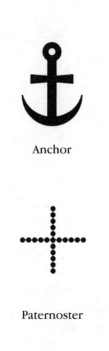

Anchor

Cross of
triumph

St James's

Bezant

Chain

Cross of
Lorraine

(also used as
the symbol
of the French
Resistance
movement in
World War II)

Paternoster

St Chad's

St Julian's

Triparted

Fitcheé

Nebuleé

Mascly

The cross has taken many different forms and been interpreted in many ways throughout history and across the world. It is such an important symbol for Christians that they return to it again and again as a focus for worship and a source of inspiration. With this in mind, there is every incentive for individuals and groups to create their own versions of the cross, which for them best express their own contemporary and cultural experience of following Jesus. Here are just a few ideas that you may like to pursue and that may fit in with a particular focus or theme that is currently being explored by your group.

- A cross of CDs. Stick together the label sides of two CDs. (There are many unwanted samples sent to homes, promoting new products or e-mail servers.) Suspend a series of these CDs vertically on a thread, with two more pairs hanging horizontally (imitating a crosspiece) at either side of the vertical string. Arrange it so that when a light is shone on to it, the cross reflects the light back, so that it becomes an eye-catching focus for worship.

- A cross of words, written in various fonts and sizes and at different angles. Perhaps a particular Bible verse could be used, or you could use different languages or a mixture of languages (using different words for God, love or Jesus) to write the verse in an unfamiliar way. John 3:16 would be an appropriate verse for this type of cross.

- A cross of 'junk', made from what we normally throw away. This cross could provide a starting-point for a meditation on God's pain at seeing us spoil and lay waste his beautiful creation.

- A cross of arrows, country shapes and forms that need to be filled in. This could be a 'refugee' cross—a way of highlighting the hardship, fear and loneliness faced by many millions who have been obliged to leave their homes because of war or natural disaster.

- A cross made of materials that recall particular cultures and techniques such as:
  - Batik shapes and patterns from West Africa
  - Paper cuts on a red background to denote China
  - Patterns and geometric shapes from the Middle East
  - An origami cross from Japan
  - Festive flowers from Central America
  - Mosaic patterns from North Africa

- Although these crosses are not strictly symbols of particular Christian communities, they do express the Christian belief that God is totally involved with all of his creation and has love for people everywhere. Other crosses could be made from photos, foodstuffs or magazine pictures that relate to issues such as war, famine, fair trade issues, child labour, abuse of women and so on. Groups may like to create a cross of their own that represents their own church or school, expressing both the way it is, and as the way they hope those outside their community will regard it.

You could also make distorted cross shapes that reflect some of the social and economic injustice to be found in the world. Such crosses, having disproportionate arms and/or uprights, could represent the pain of Third World debt, the unequal distribution of the world's wealth or the burdens of war and suffering experienced in different parts of the world.

GUIDELINES FOR EVENTS INVOLVING CHILDREN

The following is a simple checklist for teams who are planning special events with children. Make sure you work through this list with all members of your team before the event.

- Ask whether there is a local church or diocesan Child Protection Policy already in place. If there is, work within its guidelines. Criminal Record Bureau (CRB) forms may need to be signed and references provided.
- Be aware of the recommended ratio of adults to children. A minimum of 8 children to 1 adult is advised for children aged 8 and over. There should be more adults if the children are younger or are doing an activity away from the usual premises.
- Children should always be accompanied if for some reason they have to leave the group. However, male leaders should not take girls to the toilet.
- Do not take responsibility for children without written permission from parents/guardians. Pre-registration forms are recommended, which should include contact telephone numbers and any medical information.
- Exits and entrances to the venue should be stewarded and all those who are leaders should be clearly identified in some way so that children know who is 'safe'.
- First-aid qualification should be held by at least one adult leader present for every 50 children at the event. Accidents should be recorded and reported to the person in overall charge.
- General, simple safety rules should be clearly set out, especially concerning movement about the building, refreshments, going to the toilet and being quiet for important announcements.
- Have a designated overall leader for the event, who takes final responsibility for safety, security and any pastoral issues that may arise.
- Insurance for the event should be checked. This may be covered either by the local church (through EIG Parishguard, for example) or by an external organization leading the event. Involvement of the Local Authority is only necessary if the event involves children aged 8 or under for more than two hours a day on six or more days a year.
- Junior leaders (under 18) should not be left in charge of any activity or workshop involving children.

CONTACT DETAILS AND INFORMATION ABOUT THE PUBLISHERS

BRF is a Christian charity committed to resourcing the spiritual journey of adults and children alike. BRF publishes Bible reading notes and books for adults and, under its children's imprint *Barnabas*, a wide range of books to resource the teaching of RE at Key Stages One and Two, as well as materials for children's leaders in churches.

BRF can be contacted at:
First Floor, Elsfield Hall
15–17 Elsfield Way
Oxford
OX2 8FG
Tel: 01865 319700
Fax: 01865 319701
Email: enquiries@brf.org.uk
Website: www.brf.org.uk

CMS is a voluntary mission agency of the Anglican Church and works in partnership with churches across the world. Through its work in Europe, Africa and Asia in particular, CMS links up the Christian family in order to promote church growth and the mutual sharing of resources for mission.

CMS can be contacted at:
Church Mission Society
Partnership House
157 Waterloo Road
London
SE1 8UU
Telephone: 020 7928 8681
Fax: 020 7401 3215
Email: info@cms-uk.org
Website: www.cms-uk.org

TEMPLATES FOR ETHIOPIAN DECORATIVE CROSSES

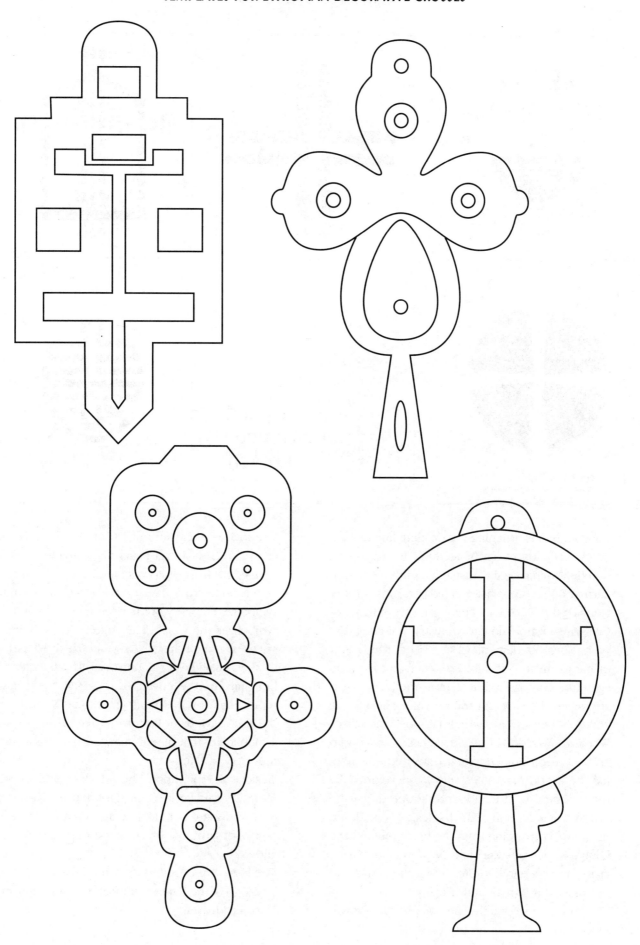

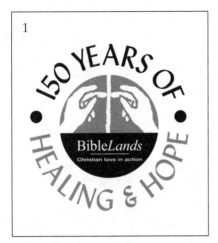

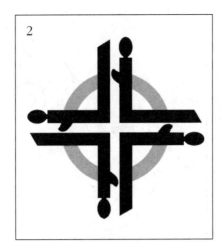

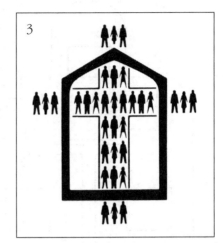

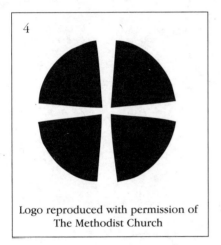

Logo reproduced with permission of
The Methodist Church

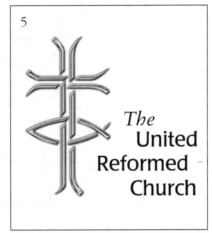

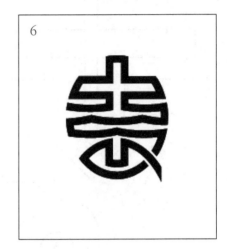

1. The two hands touching the dividing line make a cross in the logo from Bible*Lands*. Bible*Lands*, a non-denominational Christian charity working in partnership with Christian-led projects in the lands of the Bible, has been at the very heart of Christian compassionate ministry for over 150 years, since its beginnings in 1854 at the height of the Crimean War. Bible*Lands* Project Partners share the compassion of Jesus as they tend, treat and teach the sick and the needy, especially the children—regardless of their faith or nationality.

2. Women's World Day of Prayer has a cross logo created from four people at prayer. The symbol for the World Day of Prayer was developed by the women of Ireland and adopted as the international logo in 1982. Its design is made up of arrows converging from the four points of the compass, persons kneeling in prayer, the Celtic cross, and the circle representing the world and our unity through all our diversity.

3. The former logo of the British Church Growth Association.

4. The logo of the Methodist Church. The orb and cross device is a registered mark granted by the College of Arms. It consists of a red orb charged with a white cross. The cross is in radiant form to symbolize the glory of the risen Lord, and the orb symbolizes the world. The colours red and white are used: red for the orb to symbolize the doctrine of the possibility of a universal salvation for all humanity by the power of the Holy Spirit, also represented by this Whitsun colour. White is for the risen saviour of Eastertide. The whole logo is symbolic in that it summarizes the missionary message of Methodism first set out by John Wesley: 'I look upon the whole world as my parish:… I judge it meet, right and my bounden duty to declare unto all that are willing… the glad tidings of salvation. By grace are ye saved through faith.'

5. The logo of the United Reformed Church.

6. The logo of the Baptist Union of Great Britain and Northern Ireland.

Resourcing children's work in church and school

Simply go to **www.brf.org.uk** and visit the barnabas pages

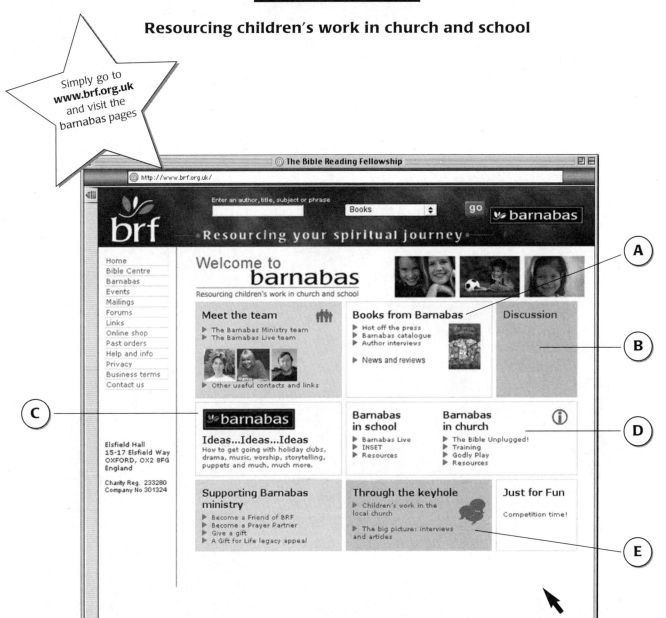

BRF is a Registered Charity

A Browse our books and buy online in our **bookshop**.

B In the **forum**, join discussions with friends and experts in children's work. Chat through the problems we all face, issues facing children's workers, where-do-I-find… questions and more.

C **Free** easy-to-use downloadable **ideas** for children's workers and teachers. Ideas include:
- Getting going with prayer
- Getting going with drama
- Getting going with the Bible… and much more!

D In the section on **Godly Play**, you'll find a general introduction and ideas on how to get started with this exciting new approach to Christian education.

E In **The Big Picture**, you'll find short fun reports on Barnabas training events, days we've spent in schools and churches, as well as expertise from our authors, and other useful articles.